The
Choice-
maker

The Choice-maker

ELIZABETH B. HOWES
and SHEILA MOON

Formerly published under the title *Man the Choicemaker*

A QUEST BOOK

*This publication made possible
with the assistance of the Kern Foundation*

THE THEOSOPHICAL PUBLISHING HOUSE

Wheaton, Ill., U.S.A.
Madras, India/London, England

First Quest Edition published by the Theosophical Publishing House, Wheaton, Illinois, a department of The Theosophical Society in America, 1977.

Library of Congress Cataloging in Publication Data

Howes, Elizabeth Boyden, 1907–
    Man, the choicemaker.

    (A Quest Book)
    Includes bibliographical references and index.
    1. Life.   2. Man.   3. Man (Theology)
4. Choice (Psychology)   I. Moon, Sheila, joint
author.   II. Title.
[BD431.H672   1977]   218   76-54 534
ISBN 0-8356-0492-6

Printed in the United States of America

To Carl G. Jung
Fritz Kunkel
Henry B. Sharman
in whose choices lie
the historical roots of this book

and to a fourth
Luella Sibbald
with whom for twenty-five years
we have learned that these truths
can in fact be lived

CONTENTS

PREFACE

It gives us genuine joy to express to several people our thanks for what they have given to the making of this book. Dorothy Phillips, editor of *The Choice Is Always Ours,* and Jack and Floy Tootell, three longtime friends and co-workers, made their way through the original material with love, care, and remarkable objectivity. Their critical judgments were invaluable. Florence Little, librarian, colleague, and book-sharer, read the manuscript in several versions, helped with all, and with total generosity gave her time and skill to documentations, bibliographical details, corrections, and to various other important matters.

We should also like to express our appreciation to Walter Wink, Associate Professor of New Testament History at Union Theological Seminary, for his active interest in and enthusiasm about our book. His suggestions and encouragements have been gifts to us.

Our gratitude is great to our manuscript typist, Doris Walker, who has worked cheerfully under time pressures and has always given her best.

The theme of this book grew over many years out of our work as leaders of seminars in religion and psychology, and as psychotherapists. To all members of seminars may we say a particular thanks for the immeasurable wealth of new ideas and fresh perceptions given to us. We also appreciate the kindness of all those who have permitted us to use, in well-disguised form, their personal material from journals and dreams.

ELIZABETH BOYDEN HOWES
SHEILA MOON

San Francisco, California

ACKNOWLEDGMENTS

Grateful acknowledgment is given to the following publishers for use of their copyrighted material:

Doubleday & Company, Inc., for lines from "A Frost Lay White in California," from *The Hazards of Holiness: Poems, 1957–1960,* by Brother Antoninus. © 1958, 1959, 1962 by Brother Antoninus.

Grove Press, Inc., for lines from "Journey," from *Stand Up, Friend, with Me,* by Edward Field. Copyright © 1963 by Edward Field.

Harcourt Brace Jovanovich, Inc., for excerpts from *The Family Reunion* and *Four Quartets,* by T. S. Eliot; excerpt from "Poem for Psychoanalysts and/or Theologians," by C. S. Lewis, in *Poems,* ed. by Walter Hooper.

Little, Brown & Company, for "The Heart is the Capital of the Mind," by Emily Dickinson, from *The Complete Poems of Emily Dickinson,* ed. by Thomas H. Johnson. Copyright 1929 © 1957 by Mary L. Hampson.

New Directions Publishing Corporation, for excerpt from "Joy," from *The Sorrow Dance,* by Denise Levertov, copyright © 1966 by Denise Levertov Goodman; lines from "What will you do, God, if Death takes me?" by Rainer Maria Rilke, from *Selected Works,* Vol. II, tr. by J. B. Leishman, copyright © The Hogarth Press, Ltd., 1960; "Danse Russe," by William Carlos Williams, from *Collected Earlier Poems,* copyright 1938 by New Directions Publishing Corporation.

W. W. Norton & Company, Inc., for lines from *Duino Elegies,* by Rainer Maria Rilke, tr. from the German by J. B. Leishman and Stephen Spender. Copyright 1939 by W. W. Norton & Company, Inc. Copyright renewed 1967 by Stephen Spender and J. B. Leishman.

Oxford University Press, for excerpt from *House by the Stable,* from *Collected Plays,* by Charles Williams.

Random House, Inc., for lines from "New Year Letter (January 1, 1940)," from *Collected Longer Poems,* by W. H. Auden. Copyright renewed 1962, 1965 by W. H. Auden.

Simon & Schuster, Inc., for lines from "Let Go. Return," from *Year's End,* by Josephine W. Johnson. © Josephine W. Johnson 1937.

PROLOGUE

Any day, each day, every day, may hold within it one or many of the questions that constitute the prods of a life. Out of night's unconscious stirrings, with the quick freshness of dawn, or in the deliberate consciousness of noontime these questions come. They are mixed always with the outer realities that move toward, away from, and around us. They are the minimal or the maximal explosions that occur whenever *I* as person encounter all that is *not-I*.

What shall I do with today? Am I free to make it (permit it to be?) something or nothing? Is this day's time sold out? Lost? Taken? What can I do to assist it toward fulfillment? What can I do with this conflict about _____? What shall I do about her who upsets me? About him who takes my strength? The negativities of my life—can I learn some means of meeting them differently? Must aggression and hostility devour me? Is there a way that they can be transformed?

These terrible opposites which pull me apart—where did they come from? What can change them from enemies to partners? Where is the integrative point? Is there a way to deal creatively with my personal and seemingly petty anxieties and also with my large, dark, fears? Where is the place within me on which I can stand in order to deal fully and creatively with my sexual urgencies? How can I learn to discriminate between the bud of a new ethic and the deadwood of old solutions? Should I be serving my own growth first? Or is the central value the good of others? How can I decide where to go or what to do to help this poor world? Can one individual—me—do anything? What does personal integrity demand?

What meaning is in the word "God"? Is it an empty word? What does it have to do with evil? With Satan? Is darkness just my invention? Or can evil, Satan, darkness, and God be seen as part of some living reality that I can relate to? If I "find my inner Self," will that help me to know God? Or if I relate to God, will it help me to find the Self in me? Can I really become whole? What is the price for that, if it is possible? What is the relationship between unconscious forces moving in me and my hard-won consciousness? Am I relevant? What is the significance of my struggle for consciousness in an increasingly inhuman environment? Is the universe evolving? Does man's self-reflection have a unique place in it? What does it involve to be truly an individual?

Where are answers to be found? Today's meaningful symbols —do they exist? Where? Are old ones still rich and living? Can they be revived? How can I create a life rooted in deep inner processes? What may I learn freshly from Jesus the Jew? Is he the same as the Christ image? Or Christianity? Does he have words to say to me? To Western man?

So the great cross-examination goes on. Life asks me questions, I ask Life. Behind all the questions, behind all variants of them, behind my existence that rests on them, stands the Eternal Question: *Man, where art thou?* Where are you going? it asks me. Where? Where are you coming from? What purpose do you flee from? Or serve? Since the beginning of recorded time, answers have been put forward. Through different histories, in different cultures, and in infinite variations of vocabulary, perhaps the single Eternal Answer remains: *Here am I!*

These questions and some particular answers are at the heart of our book. We are bringing to them a point of view articulated with urgency, concern, and, we hope, with as much objectivity as possible. In one sense, the answers we bring—insofar as they are answers—are not new. In another sense their special inter-weaving of discovered truths and still-being-discovered possi-bilities may be unique, laid on a universal ground that holds the problems of our time.

We bring to the book a double experience of over twenty-five years as analytical psychologists in the Jungian tradition, and the same number of years as leaders of seminars in the com-bined fields of religion, analytical psychology, art, and mythol-ogy. Consequently, we speak from the insights and learnings that have accrued to us during these years. A new intersection of religion and depth psychology has evolved from our work. Dr. Howes has written and studied and is working currently on further research into the Synoptic Gospels, especially with ref-erence to the psychological implications in the teachings of Jesus. The approach to the Gospels is based on sound Biblical criticism and open-minded search for what lies behind the Christian myth and its relevance for today. Dr. Moon has specialized in the religious meanings of symbols in art and litera-ture and in comparative mythology, especially in American In-dian myths.

All the values, concepts, and experimental techniques set forth here have been tried and found valuable by seminar mem-bers in the Guild for Psychological Studies during the years of work, and thus are pragmatically grounded.

We hope that we convey, in bringing together these various elements, the rich and unique contribution of Carl G. Jung to the fields of religion and theology, especially to an understanding of the heresies and of the symbols behind dogma.

In any case, each reader will ask his own questions, will cross-examine the book, and will, we hope, be cross-examined by it. If heart and mind are opened in those who move into these pages, we will be content.

PART 1

THE WAY, AND WHY

1

MAN WAS CREATED
FOR THE SAKE OF CHOICE

Confrontation with
the central fact of existence

"Man was created for the sake of choice!" If these words from
the Jewish Kabbala were taken seriously, what might the consequences be for man? What might he do differently than he is
doing with his world? With himself? Toward what goals might
he work? The words imply that man's destiny (and his planet's
destiny) is bound up with his ability to make wise choices.
This requires that he come to know himself.

"Man was created for . . ." is a statement of a fundamental
reason given in all great creation myths, in all religions, and inherent in all religious depth psychology, as to man's worth.
There is a core of meaningful process in man from the beginning, the words suggest, a possibility of man being whole that
must be realized, else he destroys his world and his kind.

But not only realized. Chosen. Choice can be made for creation, choices to fulfill that creation, choice for values inherent
not only intrapsychically but also in the outer world. Man can
be involved in implementing the values that cry out to him in
situations; he can choose to have a part in the transformation

that is needed inside him in order to become himself. For only when he *chooses* to be an implementer will he *become* one; only when he *chooses* to take the journey to find the Self will he *know* himself in the deepest sense. Choice is there because the evolutionary movement requires it, and because, through it, authentic personality is accomplished. Paul Tillich,[1] in considering the relevance or the irrelevance of Christianity, said, "What is relevant is what answers the question of what I am myself." The sense of irrelevance comes to man, Tillich went on, because he has ceased to choose, has let himself become an object to be manipulated, altered, controlled, "forced into happiness," made into a "blessed animal." And unless he comes to know, acknowledge, and choose to accept his "essential humanity," he merely exists, distorted and imprisoned, having renounced his part in creation. Thus he also renounces the central fact of his existence, and his world becomes mechanized, automatized, embattled, meaningless. He is lost in politics he cannot cope with, wars he cannot stop, history he cannot understand, alternatives he does not see.

All but the most totally unconscious among us can sense that life's moments do in fact offer alternatives for choice, whether we like it or not. Some occasions allow time for deliberation, for conscious and considered decision. Other situations arise suddenly, demanding immediate response: being held up, being accused without warning of something that is not our fault, being in a boating mishap where more than one person must be saved and you alone can swim, witnessing an accident and having to decide whether to testify. Such situations can be multiplied endlessly, small ones and large ones. And the response seems to be creative or destructive depending upon our inner orientation and the depth and quality of our awareness. The more deliberate moments represent only a small portion of man's life. Many such moments come to us as crises in jobs, careers, marriages, friendships. Here we are forced to become very aware of alternatives, usually recognizing how much depends upon what we decide and how we move. We feel the need for a dependable source for such choices inasmuch as our life, as well as other lives, depends upon how we choose.

Sudden choices are more at the mercy of our unawareness and our unconsciousness, and thus are much more easily lost as chances for creative action. Yet the fact that they make up the greater part of a man's entire life means that his neglect of them is what lies behind the depressions, alienations, futilities, and hostilities that plague us as civilized people. Man complains about his culture and its meaninglessness, about his insufficiencies in love and relationship, about his ineptness at peace. But he does little or nothing about understanding where he himself is in the whole movement of an evolving universe.

The existential situations emerge for a person not only as he becomes engaged in them outwardly but also as he becomes inwardly aware of his involvement in them. He lives in a real outer world of spontaneous confrontations and deliberate encounters with others. He also lives in an equally real world of forces and "persons," inside his own psyche, that require choices and encounters. Whether in the inner or the outer world, *nothing other than he makes the choices.* Man is the chooser. He is not given freedom. He has intentionality about freedom. In one very real sense *he is freedom.* By the very fact of being man rather than a lower animal he consists of freedom and intentionality and flexibility of response. It is as if all situations were waiting—unrealized and in need—for the free response of a unique individual to make those situations creative —that is, to have the fullest potentials of situations realized, rather than having them limited by man's egocentricities.

One action is "better" than another for the realizing of potentials. If a man has a genuine gift for leadership, actions leading toward brotherhood are better uses of his potential than actions leading men toward controlling by power and destructiveness. One may have inherited money—but he can choose how it will be used. Facts—outer and inner objects, people, interrelationships, inheritances and acquisitions—are eternally there. The vibrant charge of these facts, however, is dissipated unless a choosing human consciousness transmits it. Only human consciousness can recognize the purposiveness in neutral facts and can bring purpose into manifestation through such facts.

Pierre Teilhard de Chardin points out that man has a "Grand Option." [2] He can accept or reject the clarity of the kind of seeing that is creative. He can enter into or withdraw from the evolutionary process that moves toward ever more conscious encounters of creature with creator, of creature with creature, of creature with himself. As soon as Homo sapiens evolved and became self-reflective and capable of an expanded kind of love, the Grand Option was there for him.

It would seem that this "man" with whom we are involved, because "he" is in fact "we," is the hope of the creator for a future. What is the point of Creation, as set forth in the gathered wisdom of the world's creation myths? [3] Generally it is that a creator-god desires a creature with whom he can have communication. Sometimes the creator is lonely. Sometimes the creator is urgent for manifestation. Sometimes the creator longs to know and to be known. There are also myths where the creatures emerge out of dark nothingness, make their way upward, and come only later to a creator. In any case, at some point, even in the most primitive myths, the creature begins to be a chooser. The choices are either for or against the creator. And it is usually of vital concern and consequence to the creator which way the creature chooses, because by the creature's choices the creator "lives" or "dies," is manifested, incarnated, or not.

This matter of choice and its significance has been at the heart of religious concern for thousands of years. The primitive medicine man who helps the sun to rise is choosing to work with his creator. So is the modern poet Rainer Maria Rilke when he asks, "What will You do, God, when I die?" [4] Unhappily, contemporary organized religion has often failed to deal with choice in a living way—and thus is struggling with spiritual bankruptcy. It is possible that dead are man's God-images, because they have not included the why and the how of the relationship between man's choices and God. It is possible that, by losing vital contact with the insights from the great myths, religions, and dreams, man has lost touch with his essential irreplaceability as a conscious instrument of creative evolution.

Fortunately there are contemporaries who do not run from the fact of an Other, who see life as meaningful and purposive and related to Something beyond what would make it a mere personal "bootstrap" operation. Teilhard de Chardin [5] speaks of the Other as the Omega Point, operative within and through every molecule of the universe as the evolutionary thrust. Nikos Kazantzakis [6] speaks eloquently of the Cry struggling to be heard in each man and in the surrounding life, and speaks of God as the Cry. Carl G. Jung,[7] the Swiss psychologist-explorer of the inner world of man (and the person whose analytical psychology undergirds this book), refers to the Self as God-image to be realized psychically. Martin Buber [8] addresses himself always to the eternal Thou behind all life. Paul Tillich continually refers to the Ground of Being as a synonym for God. And in a previous time, Jacob Boehme [9] the mystic spoke of the Nothing that was desirous of becoming Something in and through man. All of these were concerned with the urgency of choice for both man and the Other. All of them have said that an apocalyptic wrath and destructiveness will be our final heritage unless our concern and urgency intensifies until it forces us into larger responsibility for choosing the greater Value above all the lesser values, both those within ourselves and in the outer world.

The fact that there are certain value possibilities which are "better" than certain others does not mean that they can be set forth as rules for, or by, anyone. They are brought to light by the true inward search and the honest outward encounter. If it is only by self-reflective relationship to Creation, inner and outer, that man can further Life, then he had best be about this relationship. Perceiving situations in the world with the intent of finding where the Cry is being sounded, where the Nothing is desperately trying to become Something, is one way. This may be in crises between blacks and whites, or in the struggles of the poor, of students, of awkward new nations. The need may be the problems of pollution or overpopulation. It may be to help anything deprived, lonely, lost, or helpless. Another way to further this Cry, this "building of Earth," is to step with courage into its *inner* dimension of our own existence.

Jung pushed the limits of this inner dimension farther and farther during his long and creative career. For him the future of mankind is deeply dependent upon how each one of us courageously undertakes this interior journey to the Self. He expressed again and again that only as the inner world is opened and made conscious can the outer world of man be saved. Unless the unconscious levels of the psyche become known, they are projected into the world outside, where they are then abated, persecuted, or adored. If we do not explore these depths, we cannot have any "imagination in evil." And if we do not have this ability to realize our capacity for evil, evil may well destroy us. Unless we include and accept our depths into our self-reflectiveness, there actually is no self-reflectiveness.

What, then, is the purpose of creation? It seems that each of us as creature is needed by creator and creation. Our choices represent our assent to this need. By our choices the worlds— our unique inner ones and our shared outer one—will take their courses. This is the central fact of existence. It requires the acknowledgment of whatever is in the psyche (Self, God-image) and whatever is in the universe that makes for wholeness and healing, whether we call it the Cry, the Omega, the Struggle, or God.

The way of choice is, in all religions, involved with paradoxes. In Oriental philosophy one must abandon desire for the achievement of tao. In myth and folktale the hero must meet obstacles, dragons, giants, barriers, evils—and often be overcome by them —before he is able to win the treasure. Jesus said that in order to have Life one has to lose one's life. In the language of analytical psychology, man must choose to go into the least liked, most inferior, darkest levels of himself if he is to have a chance of becoming whole. The dignity and creativity of such paradoxes have almost been lost in the contemporary world. We have become more and more trapped in our rational Puritan inheritance, which confidently separates what is considered "good" from what is considered "bad," places property and technology above persons, and subdues its environment into a polluted, crowded, violent chaos. Many are now caught in unthinking emotional rebellion against the too overly rational past. Choice lies lost, while evasions of choice multiply, both in man's personal life and on the national and international scenes.

No matter how it is described, this paradoxical way fundamentally involves the choice, made with as much consciousness as one can achieve at each step, of new criteria of value. It is a choice for a basic reorientation of personality, as well as of world view. It is a shift from old values based on egocentrically distorted perceptions to new values based on authentic responsiveness and greater openness both within man and in situations. Choice develops from a primitive, almost pre-choice level to the highest spiritual sacrifices. The tiny glimmerings of our human choicefulness are there from the beginning. Myth delineates this. Religious evolution as illuminated by myth reflects the growth of this small nucleus of potential humanness through the enlarging and sharpening of man's consciousness until the finest scope of the human spirit is achieved. For each man as individual this same movement is possible. The pinpoint reality of first consciousness, rooted in his basic structure, grows and grows until it becomes the ultimate determinant for the way his life can go.

The relationship between any man and the Ground of Being is the central import of the statement, "Man was created for the sake of choice." There is no better place to begin an exploration of this than with the struggles set forth in Genesis, in the mythic account of the problems of the Elohim (gods), of the Lord God Yahweh and his Adam.

Before we move forward, however, let us say that, with full awareness, we are dealing with Biblical material not only in the usual ways, but symbolically. We will examine Old Testament myths, as well as the parables of Jesus, as if they were dreams. We feel that one of the richest approaches to Biblical material is by way of this symbolic interpretation, and that much which has lost its power comes alive again in this way.

2

MAN BECAME
A LIVING BEING

*Truths in
the Garden of Eden myth*

To move into myth is to move into the existential world of tries and failures, into the strange place where one can see (is shown) the nature of beginnings and of repetitions. A myth tells of things as they are in the spiritual-psychic dimension. It reveals the structure of that reality. It sets forth the unconscious in its universal collective aspect and thus unveils a mystery that is essentially religious as well as psychological. As Mircea Eliade writes, "the religious experience is at once a total crisis of existence and the exemplary solution of that crisis." [10] In this sense, the creation myth from Genesis (ch. 1), our Western European and Judeo-Christian myth, is a description of the crisis of yes/no, the religious-psychological experience pertaining to·that, and the relationship to that Other without whom there can be no choosing.

The myth tells how aeons passed during which "the wind of God was moving over the face of the waters." Then that restless wind of God, that Freedom in the darkness, undertook the making of man. And "man became a living being" set down in the midst of a luxuriant and fruitful garden near a splendid fourfold river. All was well, sheltering, abundant, complete, as when life rests in the quietness and richness of the womb— a state that man longs to hold to, or to return to, eternally. And such longing eternally beclouds his acts.

Except for the fact that there was in the garden a tree of the knowledge of good and evil, everything else—including the tree of life in the middle of the garden, like a world navel—was good. Why did the tree of knowledge have to be present? Why wasn't the life tree enough? If *we* had been setting up the situation, we probably would have left one tree and let peace reign. And yet— And yet is this situation not a good description of man's tragedy and magnificence? In his beginnings, both as a species and as an individual person, by far the most dangerously creative ability he has is the ability to know, to reflect on his knowledge, and to use or abuse it by the choices he makes. The child who ventures too close to the forbidden canal and the man who splits the atom or steps on the moon are involved with the fruit of the tree of the knowledge of good and evil.

The "human" beginnings in the Genesis myth are not seen as taking place in a primeval forest or wilderness. They take place in a garden where rivers flow in a balanced order and where trees are carefully planted—which indicates, perhaps, that even infancy is more than just nature because every normal human infant has the incredible potential for self-reflection. Most humans are held gently within this garden at first, whether born into a primitive jungle tribe or into a highly sophisticated urban family. Man is the frailest of all animals. Man is so very long helpless and dependent. Under the guise of kindness or morality or survival, the knowledge of good and evil is kept from him as long as possible, although it is there at the heart of life. And there is that in his life and in him that says, "Do!" There is also that in his life and in him that says, "Don't!" But the existential problem of consciousness is that he knows but few of the alternatives which he could know, and he chooses only rarely, even when, for survival's sake, he must choose.

In the Old Testament myth, how is the man-God problem stated? Out of the swirling mists of darkness emerge the definite boundaries of the growing place with its lovely and shining peace. The Elohim (gods) made this out of the wind of their desire. They also made man. Their creature and the container for their creature rested before them in light, waiting. And the Elohim waited too. It is as if original wholeness is suspended animation—like seeds unplanted, like candles unlit. And the Elohim (gods) somewhere became Yahweh (God). The problem of this God, or Lord God, is that he desires life, living life, which involves planted seeds and lighted candles, which in turn involves seeds shattered and candles melted. The quality of sprouting inheres in the seed. The quality of burning inheres in the candle. And the knowing-to-plant, the knowing-to-light— this is the dangerous and difficult thing. It is essential, however, for the sake of the Lord God. Why else would he have pointed out to man, so near to the very beginning, that there was a tree of the knowledge of good and evil, unless he needed to have this knowledge be kindled in the heart of his creature?

Man has been described as a piece of blank chalkboard on which the environment writes, or as a "stinking vessel" of primordial iniquity to be thoroughly washed out by a grim repentance. This Garden of Eden myth gives the lie to both extremes. In it man is seen as a necessary part of a creative act, set down in a transformative enclosure (the garden) as an integral part of it. The power of knowing and the power of choosing, just as surely as the power of living, are there as givens. In the words of Kazantzakis:

> It is as though we had buried Someone we thought dead, and now hear him calling in the night: *Help me!* Heaving and panting, he raises the gravestone of our soul and body higher and still higher, breathing more freely at every moment. . . . Every word, every deed, every thought is the heavy gravestone he is forever trying to lift. And my own body and all the visible world, all heaven and earth, are the gravestone which God is struggling to heave upward.[11]

This urgent breaking open of knowledge, this burning, is harsh. The harshness is that of Life itself struggling *in a garden,* that is, in a place of tended growth and centered nurturing. Jung,[12] in his extensive writings about the sacred enclosure (or *mandala*) as a Self-symbol, indicates that this image of a center is there in each man's psyche at its beginning. A similar idea is that of Teilhard de Chardin,[13] who postulates "radial energy" (the inward teleological energy of growth in forward directions) as being part of the birth of matter itself. Unconscious wholeness exists for man, these thinkers say, as basic to his existence. And because of this preexistent possibility of wholeness, he can move forward and try to fulfill the longing of God; he can cooperate with that Other who needs manifestation.

The unconscious wholeness is shown in the art of children. A child paints a radiant sunburst, or flowerlike forms that are contained and orderly. He paints these as early as he can hold a stick or brush with paint on it. For those who have lived in snow country, or have played on damp beach sands, there are probably memories of great circles, with spokes and a hub, around which we galloped in an almost ritualized joy. It is as if the seed, its sprouting, and its flower were "known" by the child from the beginning. Thousands of children's paintings indicate that this is true.[14]

But this unconscious wholeness matures only by way of conflict and struggle.

> And the LORD GOD commanded the man, saying, "You may freely eat of every tree of the garden; but of the tree of the knowledge of good and evil you shall not eat, for in the day that you eat of it you shall die." (Gen. 2:16–17.)

Thus the Lord God focused full attention on the controversial tree.

> Now the serpent was more subtle than any other wild creature that the LORD GOD had made. He said to the woman, "Did God say, 'You shall not eat of any tree of the garden'?" And the

woman said to the serpent, "We may eat of the fruit of the trees of the garden; but God said, 'You shall not eat of the fruit of the tree which is in the midst of the garden, neither shall you touch it, lest you die.' " But the serpent said to the woman, "You will not die. For God knows that when you eat of it your eyes will be opened, and you will be like God, knowing good and evil." (Gen. 3:1–5.)

The affair of the serpent, too, was the Lord God's doing, for the serpent was from him and part of him. (Primitively, he may even have been one of the Elohim.) Each of them, serpent and Lord God, was in possession of the truth. Just before the final expulsion of the Adam from the garden, the Lord God echoed his serpent, saying, "Behold, the man has become like one of us, knowing good and evil." (Gen. 3:22.)

This unavoidable work of manifesting the potential center of wholeness is exemplified by two contemporary dreams. A woman in her forties, during a period of critical change, dreamed:

> I start down a tunnel dug into the earth. It was long and dark, like an Egyptian tomb, maybe. I went down and down. I was afraid. At one point I had to help in the digging. When at last I reached the bottom, I was in a circular room of dark earth, and in the middle of it was a Christ figure and I knelt in front of it.

A young man, at the start of his conscious undertaking of an inner search, had this dream:

> There's a huge flower stalk, bigger than life, and it's as if I was climbing up it. It has huge thorns on it, black, sharp. But way beyond me, up the stem, in the light, I see a gigantic rose blossoming.

In both dreams the center is emphasized—as the center of the dark underground, as the implied heart of the rose. In both, there is a struggle, there is good and evil, there is actual or implied resolution and wholeness.

What does all this mean for individuals? The knowing of opposites is a godlike quality, and yet if it is not to belong also to man as well as to the gods, why is it present in many creation myths from the beginning? What was the desire of the Lord God that made him point out the tree and bring forth the serpent? Is man being seen as a child and a plaything to be made sport of? Or is he seen as the only instrument by which the Lord God can come from Nothing and that Freedom of the unformed into a complex manifestation in time? In one's personal life, are alternatives "given" by some once-removed and royal parent who will, like a policeman, punish if one mischooses? Or is it that, if he chooses between alternative acts with a concern for the whole rather than a part, the whole is enlarged by him and his consciousness, as in the two dreams?

The Other lays upon every man, as the myth in Genesis tells, the task of becoming conscious, of realizing his potential, of bringing new rhythms and fresh sorrows, of upsetting the passive dependency of the womblike garden. And this "do" and "don't" of man, this ambivalence at the heart of him, is also in the Other, if the God-serpent is any clue. As if the yes/no of man's being were part of man's divinity. As if his power to know and to decide were part of the power of God.

Why does eating of the fruit of the fateful tree change everything? Because when a man has achieved this knowledge of good and evil he also has gained the knowledge that both good and evil are in him and in every situation, and that he can from then on be conscious of the difference between them. Part of the given is, then, that ethical and moral integrity stand at the center of a choiceful life—which is perhaps why the tree of life is guarded. Life as a conscious achievement is much more than life as an unconscious garden.

There is in the myth also a linguistic clue that the burden of responsibility for creation is on man as well as on the Other. Despite the fact that Genesis seems to say that the Elohim, or

Yahweh, "made" the garden, the animals, and man, in the Hebrew language there is no word for "creator." Does this perhaps tell us that the vital resource includes both Yahweh (the fatherly light side of the divine) and his alter ego the serpent (the trickster dark side of the divine)?

The Lord God, in his dialogues with Adam and Eve, and with the serpent, seems to stand on the side of a benevolent unconsciousness. He is like a parent who says: "Go straight to school and come straight home. Don't talk to any strangers. Don't stop at the soda fountain. Be sure to wear your raincoat. As soon as you get home I'll read to you and we'll have some lemonade and take a nap." On the opposite side stands the serpent, who is neither fatherly nor motherly. Insofar as he is a family member, he is rather like an elder sibling or a wise uncle who has been around long enough to know that to assert his ideas and to risk is the only way to maturity. And he says so, loud and sure. Adam tries to remain obedient, reasonable, and unconscious. It is Eve, the feminine and irrational member of the pair, who puts her faith in the risky counsel of the serpent and prevails upon her partner to do likewise.

In personal growth, as in the growth of mankind, each one of these protagonists is essential and his actions necessary. The subtle serpent pushed evolution forward. His wisdom is to make man conscious of the opposites existing at the center of individual life and the life of God. He is in the Godhead. And he is in every psyche. Without his contrary influence there would be only inert perfection. Without the Lord God there would be no containing and no nourishing and cherishing. And there would be no challenge given and no achievement demanded before the garden with its tree of life could be found again. And without every person's inner Adam and Eve, there would be no alive, limited, creaturely extension of the Other for incarnation. In the words of Kazantzakis, there would be no "free heartbeat" to storm through the "great sunless heart" of the race.

Psychologically, it is as if manifold purposiveness was expressed as creation in man, and as if there was a desire on the part of this purpose to be fulfilled in man, to be known and realized as fully as possible. And as we watch this drama in the garden unfold, it is difficult to see why the Lord God made man with the power of choice if He had no need of it from man, if He wanted dependent children or obsequious servants. Adam and Eve are the movement of purpose into the stream of time. They are the self-reflective nature, the emergent chooser, the earth-limited yes/no with all its opposites waiting to incarnate God. If the serpent in man says "Eat," and man eats without thought, no free choice has been made by man—any more than it is made if he obeys without thought the Lord God's command, "Don't eat." And in the most despairing moments of life, when nothing and no one seems to be able to help us to know what to do—at such times we feel as if we were carrying the burden of impossible choice for the entire universe.

Perhaps self-reflection begins when the serpent emerges and when his "Do" is set over against Yahweh's "Don't." Subtlety and wisdom, as well as innocence, must be incarnate if evolution is to continue either in individuals or in the race. It is possible that the serpent is the forward thrust of purpose, away from stasis to activity. And perhaps this implies that the same serpent is the "satanic" push of the spirit against the regressive pull of the *status quo* in man and in the world. (Immediately after his baptism and his sense of sonship, Jesus went into the wilderness and encountered a Satan who presented him with staggering choices between "good" and "best.") The situation in the garden is one of uncertainty rather than certainty. Yahweh became the situation of choice, became himself the Yes/No, Lord God/Serpent conflict that could only be solved by man's choice. Yahweh himself was reflected precisely *within* this conflict, and not outside it.

Both the serpent and Eve stand more on the side of the earthy, the instinctual, the irrational, and the nonconforming. They are against the establishment. Through them the decision is made to eat of the fruit of the tree of the knowledge of good and evil. With this fateful eating, man's consciousness of the

Self begins. Man begins to know that to *be* is to have to face opposite pulls and to choose between them. Freedom of choice —and so the very existence of Freedom—must be taken seriously. Our humanity is born, our mortality sampled, and the Nothing becomes Something when the choice is made for knowledge over against innocence and dependency. And yet all of us spend untold amounts of energy resisting the serpent, resisting the risks, trying desperately to stay innocent and secure in the garden. We hold on to dependence, try to avoid decisions, grasp at comforting dreams, and substitute drugs or doctrines for the hard task of choosing to know and to do.

Once Adam and Eve ate of the fruit, the entire paradisiacal climate changed. New emotions overcame them and sent them into hiding. They were aware of themselves in a new way. Certain theological opinions notwithstanding, it could not have been sexual sin that was born at this moment. Surely it was not degrading to be part of God's creation. To mirror the divine certainly was not shameful. Perhaps the only way to understand the hiding is to remember how it feels when we become for the first time aware that we are separate, different, unique— and that people are looking at us. Or to remember how it feels when a new insight comes into us, shy and tentative and perishable. Why does a child want to run home on the first day of school? Why does a young man write his love poems in secret? Because time is needed to assimilate independence. Self-consciousness makes man self-conscious. And the young man senses that his individual substance and its sexuality has to be held, honored, dignified, and protected as a mystery.

What kind of moment is it for anyone—this Adam/Eve moment—except one of evolution? Just as the myth describes a movement in the evolution of man, so do such times in an individual life describe its evolving self-awareness. With the loss of innocence and unconsciousness a sorrow/joy dimension begins, and man's first impulse is to hide. The sorrow of separation and alienation, the joy of affirmative singularity and dignity become part of him. And the role of purposiveness in relationship is known. Are not the Adam/Eve in every man the birth, in his own space and time, of the Freedom which is transpersonal? They are the bipolar choosing process in an actual life. They are the limitations of reality concretely manifested and perceived. Perhaps God becomes a free agent (Freedom) only through the mortality in time and space of any single individual who accepts his Adam/Eve choosing center. Perhaps Adam/Eve represent man's inner greatness of conflict and consciousness.

Yahweh feared that Adam and Eve, having eaten of this tree, might become godlike and live forever. So he laid upon them and the serpent the difficult conditions of going forth. It is as if the experiment of every incarnation of Freedom (God) has to take place in time and under the laws of mortality, as if Life has to be earned by way of continuing choices, sufferings, struggles. Each individual, through the progression of a life, has to fulfill Freedom in the same way. And how man rebels against this, calling the discipline of self-discovery for God's (Freedom's) sake "punishment," clinging blindly to childish ways.

So the expulsion was a "fall" into time, a "fall" from innocence into knowledge, a "fall" into evolution, where the Lord God is Process, through man's self-reflection and consciousness. Why did Yahweh not destroy his disobedient creatures? Why did he not wipe out the garden with its tree of life? Either act would have eliminated freedom. Yahweh chose to preserve the Adam/Eve, and thus both freedom and choice, although he sent them away, and he chose to leave the tree of life where it was, although he guarded the way back to it with cherubim with flaming swords.

What is implied by this? The tree of life will always be available to man, but it must be approached from the east, the place of new beginnings and sunrises. And man must win his way to it again and again for the first time, through fires of suffering, effort, discrimination. The Nothing wanting to become Something has left a bright beacon of its longing that man find the tree of life, vital center of the garden, at last. Man stands in this lonely place outside the garden. If he awakes to his situation of lostness and anxiety and estrangement, what conditions

for wise and creative actions are involved if he is to return to
the tree of life? To put it another way, what can the Adam/Eve
do to find wholeness at a new level, having chosen to make their
own decision, and so having become both conscious and estranged?

Here, rather than later, it is necessary to be clear about the
fact that there are two kinds of choice involved—one of which
has an absoluteness about it that cannot be avoided. (There are,
as one philosopher said, a thousand ways of saying no and only
one way of saying yes. If the process of growth is to be real and
complete and lead to the tree of life, a definite "yes" has to
start it off. Søren Kierkegaard called this the fundamental
Either/Or.) Either a person wobbles endlessly between the
walls of his own narrow and imprisoning egocentricities, or he
says definitively that he will go toward Life of a larger kind no
matter what is demanded on the way. This latter decision ab-
solutely determines all future choices. It is a decision *to be
committed* to acting always in the direction of the Cry, of that
which struggles in and through man for wholeness. It is a decision to stop standing outside the garden, enveloped in self-pity
and neurosis, and to move toward the tree of life with all that
one is, both known and unknown. It is a decision that must
involve as much of consciousness as a man can know and as
much of the unconscious as he can make available to himself
at the time of choosing.

After this first "yes," possibly all future decisions are, in the
very nature of growth, imperfect, questionable, sometimes right
and sometimes wrong. This does not alter the overarching Yes.
Having spoken this word (in the light of the desirability of the
fruit of life), man must begin to face what is involved in the
way itself. This means, among other things, to recognize the
importance of the development of a creative ego by which specific choices can be made. It also means to face those aspects of
the psyche usually avoided, to withstand the deeply regressive
pulls, those satanic elements that would drag a person backward into old and destructive responses.

By being put on his own to work for the Self in him, man

has the possibility of becoming, in a modest, realistic, but challenging way, a "savior of God." In many of the teachings and parables of Jesus there is a stress on the need for cooperation and mutuality between man and God. The Genesis drama gives only the first glimpses into the fact that God "creates" man because God needs man, although God in his own unconsciousness is, in a sense, not certain about what role man is to play, because evolution is not determinism. Nonetheless, it is possible for man to come to the tree of life if he will pay the price. And unless the price is paid, he resides in a kind of hell. As a contemporary poet has put it:

> Hell is the being of the lie
> That we become if we deny
> The laws of consciousness and claim
> Becoming and Being are the same.[15]

When man does return to the garden, to the tree of life, when he achieves his meaning as a microcosm of the larger Freedom, it will not be the same garden. The happening of consciousness that lies between Eden and Gethsemane is the substance of the rest of this book. It is an enormous happening. And difficult. And unbelievably rewarding because it brings man to himself and to a new relation to God. It can happen only step by step, beginning with the necessary departure from the innocence of the first garden.

3

WHAT MUST I DO?

Conditions
to be fulfilled for Life

The tree of life stands waiting, guarded by the flaming sword. In one of the dramatic scenes in Jesus' life a young man came to him and asked, "Teacher, what shall I do to inherit eternal life?" (Luke 10:25.) Jesus, in the deceptively simple way he had as a teacher, tossed the question back. And the young man replied with some Old Testament words, plus some additions of his own, "You shall love the Lord your God with all your heart, and with all your soul, and with all your strength, and with all your mind; and your neighbor as yourself." (Luke 10:27.) Jesus readily agreed with the young man that this was the way, saying that if he did this, he would live. For the young man, as well as for any of us desiring to go toward Life, there is more to these sweeping commandments than is at first evident.

First, there is the idea of "eternal life." It is important to link the ancient myth in Genesis with the urgent newness breaking through in the work and thought of Jesus. What can be said of "eternal life"? What has not been said about it during the long centuries? How can it be seen freshly so that the ancient resonances of its meanings are reawakened? Let us look at some of the final passages of a remarkable novel:

> Great are the stars, and man is of no account to them. But man is a fair spirit, whom a star conceived and a star kills. He is greater than those bright blind companies. For though in them there is incalculable potentiality, in him there is achievement, small, but actual. Too soon, seemingly, he comes to his end. But when he is done he will not be nothing, not as though he had never been; for he is eternally a beauty in the eternal form of things.[16]

The paradoxical quality of eternal life is demonstrated poignantly in many statements by contemporary individuals engaged in life-and-death struggles. Two examples may illustrate. The first is in a letter from an eighty-four-year-old woman who knew her time was limited to a year or less:

> The creator craving the co-operating companionship of the creatures and patiently and lovingly providing the experience whereby the creature [sic] may grow into understanding, creative, loving co-operation seems to me a . . . valid metaphor for the God-role.[17]

The second is from the journal of a man in his forties facing certain death from cancer within weeks:

> This whole terrible thing that is happening to me is a further turn of the screw. I keep thinking it is an awesome thing to look into the face of the living God. I feel God is turning the screws so I will get into an ultimate position of transition, but I also feel that the center of the circle is buoying me up, holding me in suspension as though I were in God's hands. And God, terrible and loving, is with me now in his presence.[18]

Jung, in pointing out that the ancient alchemists were really concerned with the "world-creating spirit concealed or imprisoned in matter," and the lapis, or jewel, being sought for was eternally present although it had to be found, wrote:

> Time and again the alchemists reiterate that the *opus* [work] proceeds from the one and leads back to the one.[19]

And, finally, there are these simple lines coming at the end of a modern poem about a man on a journey:

> . . . He didn't do anything violent as he had imagined.
> He cried for a long time, but when he finally quieted down
> A place in him that had been closed like a fist was open,
>
> And at the end of the ride he stood up and got off that train:
> And through the streets and in all the places he lived in later on
>
> He walked, himself at last, a man among men,
> With such radiance that everyone looked up and wondered.[20]

Eternal life, then, can be understood as the irreversibility of evolution; as that beauty which is in the eternal happening in the realm of the archetypes; as the simple act of walking as one-self in an everyday way but in a new radiance. Or it can be expressed in so many other ways and words. But all the ways and words seem to include the sense of ongoingness emerging from change, of a reborn, reunited state of being, of the mystery of newness in a never-ending spiral movement.

The urgency of the young man's question, "What shall I do to inherit eternal life?" is doubly great today in the face of our ecological self-destruction. If the life of the anthill slowly killing itself is all there is, then, as Teilhard de Chardin says, it is better to give up and die now. And if each man does not ask the question with the same seriousness as the young man asked it of Jesus, he is failing in the primary act of helping himself and his fellowmen to achieve a meaningful existence.

To the question "What shall I do?" Jesus' reply to the young man was in terms of action. "This do." The implication is that, in the words "love . . . with all," there is something that can be done by man. Not something to be merely believed, but something actually to be done. Certainly all the life and teachings of Jesus are filled with his actions. Love, for him, was not just an emotional belief stated in empty words. It was a responsive and responsible action. It was under voluntary control, consciously usable. It could be *done,* and it could be chosen *to be done* by anyone.

If the question of wanting eternal life is intentional, it is followed by the doing of the commands which include that enormous act, love, and those comprehensive objects of love, God, self, and neighbor. Now we are faced with a great problem. What is meant by love? Love is active, complex, urgent—a reaching for, a responding to, a sacrifice of a smaller and less valuable part for a larger and more valuable one. It is a gift given freely. In Jesus' thought, it is directed first of all and centrally toward that comprehensive One, the Lord God, already defined, among other ways, as Freedom, the Cry, Struggle.

The current religious scene has been healthily uncomplacent in many dimensions and for a good number of years. Through this upheaval, the nature of the larger Reality which is the object of devotion is being forced out of sterile unconsciousness into a new and fresh focus of concern. What is beginning to emerge is the sense that the old images of God are in fact dead, no longer able to support man's love in a meaningful way. But also what is emerging is the conviction that the Reality, God, is indeed vital.[21]

In extensive work with people in seminars over many years we have discovered that the Other, God, Purpose, Struggle (or whatever word best fits the individual experience), can be described as process which can be "known" in one of two ways: in its immanent form, i.e., as the Self or central pattern in the psyche; in its situational form, i.e., as larger meanings manifested in outer historical moments. In other words, God (or the Cry) is at work in the inner world of man as Self and in the outer world as Purpose. Both this Self and this historical Purpose reflect a transcendent process.

WHAT MUST I DO?

The several definitions already given of the Lord God are not definitions divorced from everyday reality. They are religiously existentialist. Such definitions are not concerned with "other" worlds but with this present existence and its containment of both the particular and the eternal, the "smaller than small and greater than great," the spirit and the substance, the light and the darkness. For the religious existentialist, meaning is *found* in this moment. (For the nonreligious existentialists—such as Jean-Paul Sartre, Jean Genet, dramatists of the "theater of the absurd"—meaning must be *made*. This difference is very great.) The religious existentialist can say, with Eliade, that modern man can no longer defend himself against the terror of history except through the idea of God.

Having said that man is to act positively toward the Lord God, the commandment under discussion further says that "all" must be included in this act. To use the word "all" in combination with the words "heart," "soul," "strength," and "mind," is to be almost as comprehensive about the individual psyche as is possible. "Heart" includes man's affective (emotive) energy (libido); "soul" includes those more subtle things called will, or spirit, or *élan vital,* the indwelling "divine spark"; "strength" includes the body and its physical capacities; and "mind" includes all the thinking processes. Nowhere in this commandment is there a separation between those things which are proper to offer to the Lord God and those which are improper. All is proper. All must be given in love.

It is not enough to include only those aspects of personality which are known or half known. We must also include the unknowns which nonetheless affect behavior enormously. The knowing of the all, and the giving of the all in love, are tasks that demand our best possible efforts. We must learn *how* to know but also how to reject and defeat our regressions, i.e., when we blame others for our problems, or revert to such childish reactions as sulkiness, temper tantrums, self-pity when someone cannot keep a date, etc. It is so very easy for a wife to react with hurt feelings when her husband returns home at

night in a door-slamming mood because things have gone badly
on the job. Each partner can choose—with a bit of awareness
—to regress to childish ways, or to try to bring some maturity
of response to the other. To regress in such situations is to
perpetuate alienation. To act to overcome the regression is to
learn something about love.

What is done with "all" depends upon how the ego operates,
and in whose interests. By the ego is meant the "I." It is the
center of consciousness, having emerged in childhood out of the
unconscious world of images and dreams. During its struggles
with the oughts and shoulds of childhood it is unavoidably distorted and corrupted to a greater or lesser degree so that it does
not serve the larger interests, but turns only upon its own small
center. And then we are egocentric, facing the world with blinders on, not open nor perceptive of reality either within or without. But man needs to know the real "you" who is to love with
all, and who can inherit eternal life. Otherwise he is involved
in maintaining a rigid set of egocentric images that his milieu
and his response to it have built into him as right. Thus he is
caught by these images and cannot afford to love. The real ego,
on the other hand, makes it possible for us to know the other
parts of ourselves by helping us to shed these false partial
images. The real ego, unlike the defensive ego-centered ego,
can slowly learn when to be active and discriminating in the
world of consciousness and daily life and when to permit the
unconscious to speak. When both conscious and unconscious
parts act together, genuine life and love are possible.

We must move away from egocentric and destructive anxieties
toward that fuller awareness referred to as "eternal life" by the
young man who questioned Jesus. His question we would therefore paraphrase as follows: What conditions must I fulfill so
that I can live in the present moment with fullness of response,
with all of myself? What can I do in order to move into the flow
of events with a sense of purpose? How can I feel myself, at
least much of the time, to be in the timelessness of true being?

The despair of nonreligious existentialism stands at the opposite pole from the consciousness of the possibility of eternal life. This kind of despair is obvious today among so many people, of all generations, who say, as a gifted student said: "What's the use? Nobody cares about anything but his property, how to make money, be a success, and to hell with everything that gets in the way. Some of us think that life doesn't have to be that way. But we get pushed down." He was pleading for total responses to authentic meaning. Total response (which we have described as loving with all of the heart, soul, strength, and mind) comes from a state of desire for Life, from a sense that this Life is available, and, above all, from a willingness to respond nondefensively to Life. That Luciferian principle of egocentricity leads man into rigidity, narrowness of outlook, estrangement, and far, far, indeed, from the condition of love.

4

MY NEIGHBOR
AND THE SELF

Why there are
two commandments

When an individual enters into the state of love that dominates the first commandment, he moves into a new God-man relationship. Man's answer to God's love for man is expressed in man's struggle to return to the tree of life. It is also expressed as the second commandment says, in his love for his neighbor and for the Self.

It is unfortunate that too often religion has imposed the injunction that our neighbor should always come first—unfortunate because it has implied that even if we couldn't respond to or accept ourselves, we could at least respond to or accept our neighbor. Which is of course ridiculous and impossible. As the world grows more crowded and more hostile, it seems increasingly clear that self-rejection leads to defensiveness which, in turn, leads to rejection of the other. Insecurity and hostility go hand in hand. The loving answer to God and to neighbor comes only from those who are creatively disposed to themselves. There are few obstacles that keep one more effectively from finding Life than that deeply ingrained Christian attitude that we should "forget" ourselves. This altruism, unselfishness, or self-effacement, actually may cover up a mountain of selfishness and self-centeredness. It also smothers positive value. Precisely because the need for self-fulfillment is at the core of our being, we have to turn our attention to it. Otherwise, this basic need of man and the energy it contains are first diverted and then inverted into egotism, psychological auto-eroticism, and masochism. Against such manifestations Christianity often rightly protests. But Christianity has failed, by and large, to distinguish these symptoms from their causes, and thus has been turned aside from giving attention to the causes. The elements of the real Self have been therefore too frequently neglected and even lost. Our concern is turned outwardly toward others *as a substitute* for the task of transforming ourselves. Rabbi Joshua Liebman [22] made the point that it is ironic to note that two thousand years ago it was assumed that if a man loved God, he also of course loved himself, whereas today every therapist and every minister knows that self-hatred and self-rejection are the commonplace neuroses even when the "loving" God is taken for granted. Why is this so? It seems to be that, because of his uprootedness and alienation, man is unable to love God with all because he is estranged from so much of his all. Consequently he is unable to love all of himself, and he certainly cannot love all of his neighbor, not to mention being unable to love all of his neighbors! It is possible that some of the younger generation, in fumbling toward "togetherness," may in time open up wider potentials for love of Self and neighbor. As yet, it is too soon to know if they can survive better than previous generations.

What is the psychological importance of adding the second commandment to the first? Why does that which is to be done in order to find Life have to include love of God, then love of Self, then love of the neighbor? And if love is, as Buber says, *"the responsibility of an I for a Thou,"* [23] then the I must be responsible not only for the eternal Thou, but for a neighbor-Thou, and for a Self-Thou.

If God is to be loved with *all* the heart, soul, strength, and mind, then it is clear that all these parts of Self must be discovered so they can be used in the *centralizing act* of responsibility. As parts of the Self are found, so also is the Self found as a unitary factor behind them, and when the Self is found, it is not projected onto a neighbor. A neighbor who is not used for projection can be loved.

God is included in the individual psyche and in the neighbor's also. Jesus said the Kingdom is within. Nowhere in contemporary thought has this been more urgently stated than by Teilhard de Chardin, who was convinced that only by way of a deepened knowledge of the nature of persons (psychogenesis) and by planetization (the interrelationship between all persons everywhere) could mankind carry forward in the evolutionary process.[24] If the larger Consciousness is to be furthered, he believed, it has to include Self-consciousness and other-consciousness as well as God-consciousness. Indeed, it not only has to, but inevitably will, as evolution continues.

Jung is the only depth psychologist whose concepts make man in a very real sense social before he is individual. That is to say, the archetypal world of inner images, the "collective unconscious," is considered by Jung to consist of "inherited predispositions" to behavior—man's connection to his primeval past. Thus it is "social." As the child grows, his "personal unconscious" builds up by way of his milieu, but it is secondary. The Self as God-image is there from the beginning, and has to be discovered and worked on if man is to be whole. Fritz Kunkel postulated the infant-child as beginning in a preexistent "We," primitive and unconscious. This idea is not unlike the Oriental one of the "jeweled island" there at birth, soon lost, and to be regained in maturity by work. Kunkel said that man had to lose the "primitive We," and work through lonely struggle to a "mature We."[25]

One beautiful example of the presence of this social as well as personal level of being is an example given by Frances Wickes. A six-year-old child dreams:

> There was a big-big woman and she had all the world inside her stomach, everybody in all the whole world. And she opened the door in her stomach and told me I could go in too. But there I was inside her stomach—and then I walked in and there I was.

"The child naïvely accepted the fact that she was inside the stomach of the Great Mother and outside in the world at one and the same time. It couldn't be so and yet it *was,* and she knew it because it happened and she was there. The dream said so. . . . The wisdom often known to the child who is closely connected with unconscious images fades, and in its place comes acquired knowledge." [26]

The two great commandments being considered, then, force man into a series of actions none of which can be omitted. Man responds to (is responsible for) whatever larger Meaning and Purpose he subsumes under the word God; he carries out this response with everything in his psychic structure; therefore, he works to know ever more deeply and widely this totality which makes up the psyche. As he knows this Self, accepts it, responds with love to it, he is then able to move into the outer world less defensively, more freely. The *centralizing act* is then completed because he has brought the world "within" and the world "without" into the framework of the selfsame "Kingdom of God." Through this centralizing act he moves from what Eliade has called "profane time, which is without meaning," into "sacred time"—which comes only "when the individual is truly himself." [27] That time is "sacred" which includes "infinity" and the "eternal." And these cannot be really included unless the all of the Self is involved.

After the young lawyer had asked, and answered for himself, the question about eternal life, Jesus told the following story:

> A man was going down from Jerusalem to Jericho, and he fell among robbers, who stripped him and beat him, and departed, leaving him half dead. Now by chance a priest was going down that road; and when he saw him he passed by on the other side. So likewise a Levite, when he came to the place and saw him,

passed by on the other side. But a Samaritan, as he journeyed, came to where he was; and when he saw him, he had compassion, and went to him and bound up his wounds, pouring on oil and wine; then he set him on his own beast and brought him to an inn, and took care of him. And the next day he took out two denarii and gave them to the innkeeper, saying, "Take care of him; and whatever more you spend, I will repay you when I come back." (Luke 10:30–35.)

This famous and often misinterpreted parable deserves a fresh approach from an inner point of view in addition to an outer one. Surely we are aware, or need to be, how people fail to respond when they know that fellow humans are being brutally assaulted. What keeps us from stopping to help a motorist in obvious trouble? Why can we not reach out freely to another to comfort a grief or share loving joy? What makes us often back away from the direct feeling expressions of children?

The answers to these questions and others like them are not to be found in a set of outer ethical rules. They are found through trying to understand what—or who—*within* us is the wounded part, the robber, the priest-Levite, and the Samaritan. If a person can see what he does to himself, there is some chance that the outer world will begin to change in the direction of love.

This parable is a description of certain aspects of the "journey of the soul" told by way of symbols.[28] Because symbols continually reveal eternal realities of the human situation, whether in parable, myth, classical tale, or dream, it is justifiable to deal with Jesus' parables symbol by symbol, as if they were dreams.

In the midst of this twilight dream scene, then—somewhere on a lonely and rocky road between two busy cities—lies a man, wounded and naked. His assailants are like half-glimpsed and shadowy figures. We know they have been there only because the man has been beaten and stripped of everything. All is divided and split. The part that has done the beating has fled from the part that has been beaten. The victim has been divided from health and possessions. Jericho and Jerusalem are far apart. The robbers are divided from, and are also divisive within, society.

Here is the condition of estranged man. This is how it is with him in his unhappy loneliness. One part of him has become hurt, angry, hostile, autonomous, out for its own way. It has been caught in the pressures of what ought to be, and has rebelled violently. And in its aggressive reactions and its demands for what it has not achieved, it inflicts cruel and almost fatal hurts on another part that had been trying to go forth on its journey. The journeyer is crippled and the non-journeyer is in flight. The time is dark and difficult.

If we reflect upon this as our dream, perhaps we can begin to understand it better. Our wounds are there because of the split within us, and in the very heart of our existential situation. Through the wakeful nights we feel them throbbing with pain. We feel them in our sense of abandonment, of lostness and suffering. A person who was struggling with this kind of estrangement dreamed:

> On my table I saw a large book titled *The Plunder of Time,* by Satan.

To the dreamer, this referred to the lost time of childhood, the lost joys, and also to the demonic robber, "ought," who had left the child wounded and joyless.

A young man, just beginning to see how his wounded side had to do with his dark emotions which he had felt he ought to hold back because of a strict father, had this dream:

> The southern tip of South Africa is in flames—burning because of refusal to move and change with demands of the times and refusal to integrate the dark other. Something about plunging into the Cape of Good Hope. Was it too late?

Or this dream of a woman who never allowed herself to appear weak:

Someone I know is taking care of a subnormal child, in order to help it and other children. I am introduced to this helping by being shown a little girl who wets her crib and I am to care for her.

The wounded man in the parable, then, can be our own lost childhood joys, or all of our dark African continent, or our small imperfections, or many other elements in us that have suffered because of physical or psychological cruelty. The wounded one can also be recognized in minority groups, even in nations. One group or one nation or one group of nations becomes the "robber" and another the "wounded." If we go deeper, we can begin to see, behind the social ills we decry, our inner aggressor—Satan, the "white man," the one who abandons children. Perhaps then we can begin to understand more deeply the priest-Levite as well as the Samaritan. Too often this parable has been taken as a description of how man "ought" to behave toward his fellowman. But if he sees himself as a "good" Samaritan, he is in danger of falling into self-righteousness for the very reason that he thinks he has avoided being self-righteous. If he sees himself as a "bad" priest or Levite, he is apt to end with the cry, "But how do I become a Samaritan?" We cannot become a good Samaritan merely because we think we ought to be one—or even because we truly desire to be one. Unless we can understand the attitudes of priest-Levite inside ourselves, and understand the sources of such attitudes, we will continue to "pass by" that which needs us. And we will not only pass by the outer wounded ones, but generally first we will turn away from and pass by the deep inner hurts.

Priest and Levite are good and acceptable men, upright, necessary to society, protectors of rules and of laws, carriers of tradition. They are guided by rational, good goals and ideas. They have exceedingly busy schedules. But where does all this lead them? It leads them into partialness, because they do not want to relinquish their specific goals, plans, rules, "good works," and efficient organization. To hear the cry in the night, to stop and attend the robbed and wounded, would demand more sacrifice than what they feel it is right to give. It would require time and effort. It might involve danger, both from the robbers who could return and from possible contamination from contact with "outcasts." We can see them inside us—even if we have not named them. We pretend that something done to us doesn't hurt—in order to be the "good" stoic. We try always to be courageous, hardworking, undaunted—so that people will think we are "wonderful." We conform to hateful things in order to be praised. That in man which says that to look at inner hurts is to be selfish, that is the priest-Levite. That in man which puts roles above reality, which refuses to be involved in pain, which "plays it cool," is defensive, is impatient—that is the priest-Levite. That in man which refuses to be an "I" and therefore has never encountered a "Thou"—that is the priest-Levite. That in man which follows religious conventions but which has no relationship to religion in the sense of "binding together"— that is the priest-Levite. And dreadful though the robbers seem, can they be called more dangerous in their badness than the priest and Levite in their goodness? Badness cannot utterly destroy, goodness will not heal, and the wounded hangs between, waiting. Waiting in the world, waiting inside man, waiting for what? For the Samaritan.

Why was the Samaritan able to hear the cries and respond when those who should have did not? In the time of Jesus the Samaritans, being a mixed people, were considered outcasts by the devout Jews, and were held therefore to be inferior and to be shunned. Yet only this man of Samaria took responsibility for the wounded one. Why? Perhaps he could respond because nothing held him back—no role to protect, no defensive fears, no haste to arrive somewhere, and no hectic rushing about. Perhaps also it was because for so long he had known his own suffering and, instead of ignoring it, had learned to accept it compassionately. For each person there is some part inside which, although it was hurt and rejected, does not run away from the hurts but faces them, suffers with and through them, and does not let them go underground. When some aspect in us once accepts wounds and tries to assimilate and transform them, it becomes in us a Samaritan to help hurt parts both in us and in other people. This inner helper remembers what hurts are like, and what it is to be healed. And this Samaritan in us, this healing principle, matures by the facing of wounds, small as well as large, without repressing the anguish of them. If a person can do this, not only does this inner Samaritan develop, but also his inner healing power increases, as does his relationship to inner and outer neighbors.

In fact, the development of the inner Samaritan is not far from what Jung said about personality:

> Just as great personality acts upon society to alleviate, liberate, transform, and heal, so the birth of personality has a restoring effect upon the individual. It is as if a stream that was losing itself in marshy tributaries suddenly discovered its proper bed, or as if a stone that lay upon a germinating seed were lifted away so that the sprout could begin its natural growth.[29]

"Genuine responsibility," wrote Buber, "exists only where there is real responding. . . . He who ceases to make a response ceases to hear the Word." [30] The Samaritan heard the pain, and in responding to the pain he heard the Word of God. He alone heard the Word of God singing through the hurt. So the tenderness and the mercy belong to us as well. Under the beatings and robbings of our hostility a good portion of our being falls. And a good portion of our being chooses to ignore this crippling or dying. It is an aspect of our greatness, however, that one portion remains which has learned and grown under the sufferings of existence and which desires above all else that wholeness be the state of the inner land. Not the egocentricities, not the goodness, not the adaptations—none of these can act in us from love. The Samaritan can. Thus he can be spoken of in the words of the psalmist, "The stone which the builders rejected has become the head of the corner." (Ps. 118:22.) Only the despised and rejected side can risk the merciful response, for he has nothing to lose except the divided land filled with suffering. Only the Samaritan was willing to pay the whole price, to go the entire way to achieve healing. He paid not only for the needs of today but for those of tomorrow as well, making his commitment to healing a priori. Wholeness either of body or of psyche can never be achieved by man deciding from day to day whether to work for it or not. Unless he is dedicated to it *now and in the future*—as the Samaritan was dedicated to the healing of the wounded man—it is not likely to happen.

The question of how we can find the Samaritan within us remains. Sometimes it must first be seen functioning in another person before it can be found inside—as in the example of the patient who said to the psychotherapist, "It is healing to me to know you care, and are concerned about my life." Only later could this person's own inner Samaritan be discovered. The robbers in the story are never caught. Perhaps they never are. Perhaps in us they never are. Perhaps they remain always as threats from the dark places of man's anger and terror. And always man can choose between either ignoring their destructiveness or acting with passion (compassionately) to heal the wounds they have caused, wounds within himself, wounds within the suffering world. It is somehow less demanding to see ourselves outside ourselves, to identify the robbers as those persons or nations who exploit others. Even the wounded are usually seen as the others who are afflicted—not as part of ourselves. The priest-Levites are other people who don't care about other people. And the Samaritan is seen as an outer savior.

One of the outstanding things in the teachings of Jesus is that he never says "I am the Samaritan." Just before he told the Samaritan story, he said to the man who had quoted the two commandments, "Do this, and you will live." Jesus is indicating that part of the doing is a loving of Self which is an extension of the love of God and which issues in the love of the neighbor. It is the Samaritan within who can penetrate into personal existence "with active love" and so hallow it. Do we love our neighbor? To the degree that we love the Self. If we love and hallow the Self, then surely we do love our neighbor. Because the first commandment has become split off from the second, because God has become split off from the psyche, true Self-love has fallen into the abyss. The havoc resulting from the Christian equation "self-love = selfishness" has been incalculable. Because our psyche has not been included in total love, it has been treated as an "it" instead of as a "Thou"—as the priest and Levite treated the wounded. Hating ourselves, therefore separating ourselves from the source of love and mercy, we try vainly to find and feel compassion. Perhaps this very condition of estrangement from the source of love is one of the major causes of ineffectual social action. All the outer good works in the world, if done while the inner wounded one lies ignored and bleeding, will not remove the hurts from the inner country.

5

A SINGLE CONTINENT

*Ambivalence and
the religious function of the ego*

After the "fall" from unconsciousness (expulsion from the Garden of Eden) the individual is faced with the long struggle to learn who he is, to find that center from which he can respond to life without fear, to make his way back to the tree of life—not as a crying child but as a courageous adult. It is a journey that requires patience, the willingness to learn, and the humbleness to understand that man is both single and divided and that he must encompass multiplicity and unity together.

The optimum state was described by Emily Dickinson:

> The Heart is the Capital of the Mind—
> The Mind is a single State—
> The Heart and the Mind together make
> A single Continent—
>
> One—is the Population—
> Numerous enough—
> This ecstatic Nation
> Seek—it is Yourself.[31]

Whether or not the poet's meaning of the "single Continent" referred to the Self as we use the word, she was referring to a state that could never have been found in the original garden. The primordial, permissive, sustaining initial garden (with its potential Self) allows man's life to move through the gentle seasons unconsciously. Man cannot seek the single continent with its population of one unless he leaves these early egoless and irresponsible worlds behind. As he grows from childhood he develops an "I" that makes choices, for better or for worse. And the reason choices are more often for the worse is that, in addition to the "I," or *ego,* there are backward and forward pulls within the psyche so strong as to leave the ego bewildered and incompetent.

But the Adam/Eve in man begin in the garden even though they have to depart from it. They, as well as we, have their roots in the deep unconscious beginnings. Adam/Eve, although having to accept everyday reality, nonetheless are grounded in the garden as their source, as well as having the garden as an object of deep longing. Jung describes the Self as an inner psychic reality that is at once unified and multiple, a central given of existence, a potential in man at birth. It is the *imago Dei* in man. It is universal and transpersonal, but it manifests itself in each individual singularly. It contains all elements and all opposites and yet is a unit. Thus it is from within this all-inclusive Self that many of both the forward pulls toward growth and the backward pulls toward regression come.

The ego (I) grows as we grow, being shaped and bounded by the early environment and the significant people in it as well as by individual temperament. At any given time, the ego is the focal point of consciousness, is the sum of what we would include knowingly about ourselves in such a statement as "I am not going to do that." The ego is the process of choosing, among other things. It is saying and meaning "I will." And, although the ego as choicemaking process is not the single continent, it is essential to that continent. Thus in order to act singly, man needs a religious relationship to his ego, through his ego to other parts of himself, and to the Self as potential to be realized. In a statement made to one of the authors, Emma Jung said: "There are egos and egos and egos. The problem is to find the right one."

Behind Mrs. Jung's statement is a great complexity. The problem of finding the "right one"—the real ego, the essential I—is a problem of continual development throughout much of a lifetime. There are, to be sure, crucial and often dramatic turning points when a choosing center is spotlighted—i.e., the crisis choices of adolescence, or the later life choices that Erich Neumann [32] has described as "centroversion," i.e., a mature action of the ego toward individuation. For the most part, however, the real ego grows to be clearly outlined and strongly based as one's "I-ness" slowly responds to each outer fact; and as "I-ness" becomes less contaminated by, and more detached from, unconscious contents, it responds to genuine inner facts, thus further strengthening the real ego. And the more essential "I-ness" risks encounters with inner and outer reality, the more clear, flexible, and strong it becomes as the instrument of conscious religious choice. One of the authors has dealt at length with this matter. [33]

Yet when the essential "I-ness" interacts with all the combinations from the inclusive land of the larger Self, the single continent often seems far from single. We have only to recall the previously discussed opposites in Eden. Man is tempted, as a humorist once said, "to mount his horse and ride rapidly in all directions." Dynamic opposites do exist. The tension of living substance depends upon this. In many creation myths other than Genesis this tension is symbolized. For example, in the story told by the Yokut Indians of California:

> There were several creators. Eagle was the chief one and Coyote made a lot of mistakes and did some ridiculous things, but he brought about some very good things also. [34]

Or this example, from a Mission Indian creation story, of a dialogue between the sky (Tukomit) and the earth:

Tukomit said, "Who are you?"

"I am stretched out; I am extended; I resound; I am earth-quake; I revolve; I roll—who are you?"

"I am night; I am inverted over you; I am the arch of heaven; I cover; I seize, I devour."

"Brother!"

"And you are my sister, the Earth." [35]

From these opposites, man was born. In much the same way that electrical energy is polarized, so also is psychic energy. Aniela Jaffé shows how this discovery of Jung's has begun to influence physics and biology.[36] This process of polarization is fundamental to all psychological activity, including that of the ego, not in abstraction but in the affairs of every day.

If two poles of opposed energies are basic to existence, then there are forever before man alternative possibilities for the ego's action. The hard fact is that these choices of values are rarely clear-cut, rarely black and white, but present themselves in an infinite variety of grays. In addition to *bipolarity* there is *ambiguity,* the fuzzy edge of choice that we must work to make clear. The ability to tolerate ambiguity has been named as one of the important characteristics of a mature person. Adam and Eve knew ambiguity. And their struggle included also *am-bivalence*—conflicting desire rather than fuzziness of choice.

How do these bipolarities, ambiguities, and ambivalences show themselves in the personal symbolic processes? All of us know times of indecision, of wavering, of on-the-one-hand-but-on-the-other-hand behavior—and we know also that these are emotional times of stress and often of physical fatigue or illness. Such difficulties show clearly in dreams. For example:

There were two little boys, about four years old. I hugged them to me and said, "You are my little boys and I have neglected you." One of them had a red, round spot on his face where I had previously slapped him to make him go away. I lied to him, and told him that I hadn't meant to slap hard—that I had thought there was a screen in the way to protect him. But the screen had in fact been there, and I had slapped hard to

get through it. I hoped that he would believe me, as now I was
penitent and wanted both him and his neglected brother to be
with me.

This woman obviously wanted to include the initial, neglected,
young, lively parts of herself, but was ambivalent about facing
up to her own cruelty of trying to get love with lies.

Here is the dream of a man who was torn between the life of
the spirit and the life of the flesh, with a tendency to try each
one in an extreme way.

> There is an old man dying, and he is bound, shrouded, and
> put in an open coffin together with various objects, including a
> large candy bar. I ask if the candy bar is necessary. He says, "I
> want that to eat when I come out. But it doesn't matter," he
> adds in a sort of peeve. I get the candy bar into the limited
> space by breaking it. I stay by him and wait. He is to struggle
> and give up the ghost, a relinquishing of the will finally.
>
> "You're afraid of your Father's commitment." This is the
> line I wake up with, as if repeated.

The dreamer said that this last line was "almost an interpretation" telling him what the real religious challenge was,
pointing out his ambivalence. He felt that the dying one was his
"old" way of wanting sweets and indulgences even in his
"spiritual" experience. A death struggle had to go on so that this
childishness could change from egocentricity to an ego committed to the larger Meaning ("Father"). The dreamer wanted
this change yet feared it.

Ambivalence is the longing to go forward and the opposed
longing to go backward existing in us simultaneously. It is the
right hand and the left hand wanting to do different things.
It is progression against regression. Even in the Self as center
there is a regressive pull. Man has the Grand Option to choose
for evolution or for destruction. And in Eden one side of the
divine said, "Stay where you are," while another part said,
"Take a chance."

It makes a real difference whether the serpent in Eden (or

Satan, as it eventually became) is seen as evil, or as a challenger
to consciousness. In the greater part of the Old Testament, and
in the teachings of Jesus in the Synoptic Gospels, Satan continues to be an aspect of the divine that serves to prod and
push toward creation, and thus is related to the ambivalent
trickster figures in mythology. God is described over and again
in the Old Testament as containing both darkness and light,
wrath and love, justice and mercy. And perhaps it is precisely
in this ambivalence between opposed forces that God has meaning. It is as if a totally benign Power, which never pushes man
and which treats him as an infant, does not have the vital reality
of a Power that can be wrathful as well as supportive, a Power
that, as the Jewish Midrash put it, needs man and his essential
"I-ness" to help the Lord God overcome wrath with love, and
temper justice with mercy.

Man cannot evade choice and at the same time achieve meaningful life. In order to come to maturity he needs not only to
learn to tolerate ambiguity but also to act in spite of it. Behind
and beyond all ambivalences and ambiguities is the demand
that he face and deal with all that he is aware of in the situation
and then make the best decisions he can. However, bipolarity
cannot be utilized nor ambiguity and ambivalence be resolved
without "I-ness," i.e., without the essential ego. This ego gathers
facts that are relevant to a particular situation. It faces outer
realities as well as inner ones. And at any moment the "No"
may outweigh the "Yes" unless there is something that can
confirm and affirm. Without the ego, the Self as the inner God-
image cannot be brought into participation with choice. The
ego, as Jung sees it, is oriented not only toward past and
present (as Freud conceived it) but also it must be involved in
the progressive and purposive tendencies of the psyche.

Fritz Kunkel, far ahead of his time and not well known in
this country, wrote several books on the development and
neurotic functions of egocentricity.[37] His thought stems from
that of Alfred Adler, but goes beyond Adler's into a wider
teleology that is well seasoned with wit as well as wisdom. He

points out that as soon as the Eden of infancy is left behind
and man is cast out into a less dependable environment, he begins to feel exposed and naked, and desires to be covered. For
each individual, no matter what sort of "home" he lives in, this
will inevitably be true. Each one, as he begins to say "I"
(around three years of age), unconsciously but very surely
shapes that "I" so that it will protect him from too many hurts.
If his immediate world frowns on his emotions, his "I" will act in
an unfeeling or indifferent way. If his family always rewards
success, his "I" will strive for success, or, if that isn't possible,
the "I" will try to become popular. There are many major patterns of egocentricity and almost as many variations of pattern
as there are people, and usually by the time a person has
reached late adolescence he is already in possession of an arrogant ego which, rather than freely serving a creative energy (as
was its original destiny), is unilaterally unrelated, sterile, and
destructive.

In a play by Charles Williams, the character Man is asked by
Pride for "that old jewel your servant talks/ often of—more
often than becomes him./ Soul, he calls it, I think." Man replies,
in part, ". . . if/ever such a thing was, it has been tossed/ one
day away in a corner of the house and lost./ . . . I do not
know; my paradise is I." [38]

What a succinct statement of the egocentric condition! And
before any flexible use of a creative ego can be developed, we
have to work our way out of this jungle (or desert) of ego-
centeredness. Consequently the need is to begin where we are,
namely, in the midst of what we have made into a pseudo Eden
and its remarkable variety of "I wants." The need is, to put it
another way, to face our unfulfilling but desperate efforts to
maintain this pseudo Eden, in an attempt to understand at least
some of our ego defensive patterns.

Power-demand is one of the most conspicuous patterns. When
we behave as arrogant, exploitative, managing persons who
"want what we want when we want it" we are power-demand
people. We will generally exert pressure of one kind or another.

We demonstrate little or no sensitivity or outreach toward others. Cruelty or flattery are equally effective stratagems by which we achieve our power and push our will. "Apple-polishing" and "steamrollering" are both effective.

Defensive insecurity as an egocentric pattern has a very different character. It is manifested in us when we are anxious and tense, and are either building fortresses to hide in or filling in the cracks in existing fortresses. We are the "bristlers," the easily hurt and hostile, the solitary ones, the "people are bums" man, the "don't let anyone know" woman.

Timid withdrawal is quite unlike the two preceding egocentric patterns. It is the most passive. It is manifested in us when we are eternally apologizing, self-effacing, and downgrading ourselves. Unfortunately it often looks like gentleness, and is able to evoke feelings of helpful pity from others—for a while, at least.

The Apple polishers and the Apologizers tend to elicit helping responses from others, whereas the Steamrollers and Bristlers tend to call forth opposition and/or rejection. No matter what the egocentric condition, however, its climate is entirely humorless. (We, or others, may laugh *at,* but none laugh *with.*) And no matter what our type of egocentricity may be, we are building upon a fear of life's negatives (present in the very nature of reality) and upon an unwillingness to face what Kierkegaard called "the alarming possibility of being able." We flee the negative and deny the positive, not only in the outer environment but in the inner. In the same way, as we try to manipulate, deny, repress, or distort outer events, so we do also with unconscious images and processes.

Of course choice is nonexistent when the ego is covered over with its defenses. The single continent sinks beneath the waters. The "I" is overwhelmed by fatal determinism and no new, free, spontaneous elements can break through and come into play. A core of rigidity keeps man from assuming the fearful and fruitful responsibility for his own life and he dares not risk being seen, by himself or others, imperfect and mortal. And as neurosis grows in magnitude so does egocentric anxiety. Various kinds of anxieties have been described by Kierkegaard, by Tillich, by Kunkel, by Erich Fromm, by Karen Horney, among others. Perhaps here we need only remember that one of man's deepest needs is to recognize that he did not only leave the garden, but that he then immediately made for himself a prison, and he is made aware of this, fortunately, by the anxiety, restlessness, and revolt of the imprisoned aspects within him. Thus neurotic pain may be the very thing that pushes man toward healing and wholeness.

This same ego which, when centered on itself, defensively leads to neurosis, also leads toward growth when it centers on something larger and more all-inclusive than itself. It becomes self-reflective and dedicated. Even at those crucial points where we are faced with egocentric unrealities there is a choice possible—to see or not to see. And that which must choose to see is blood brother and twin of that which is to be seen! The essential ego that lies behind the manifestations described above must decide to reflect upon itself. Then it must decide whom to serve.

At the risk of oversimplification, let us set forth three basic functions of the essential ego rooted in the Self. First, it sees outer reality accurately, free from distortion, false demands, and projections. It can thus perceive truth as the scientist can, quite objectively, and it can also, as the scientist does, select from the various alternatives that one which seems most to resemble reality. Only then is true choice possible.

Secondly, the essential ego, in contrast to the egocentric ego, is able to find and react to all sorts of symbols as statements of reality. This ego function is perhaps less thought about but it is equally important. How does the ego respond to such symbolic representations of mysterious meaning? Such familiars as cross, flag, baby, tree, candle—any of these can become symbols, eternal pointers toward ever-changing reality. Most people do not have egos that are so flexible and expansive. Nonetheless, many people show that a well-expanded creative "I-ness" can see not only outer real facts but also can perceive their ineffable realities in their "metaphysical moorings." Outer facts can thus be seen as more than themselves. Their symbolic significance can be grasped.

The essential ego, thirdly, is the perceiver of inner reality as well as of outer reality. That is, in addition to seeing outer things symbolically, the ego can turn itself toward such unfamiliars as dwarf, sea serpent, winged horse, faeries, and the like, and can embrace them as truths coming from the land below the rational. Here the ego performs one of its most important tasks—relating these two worlds. If the symbolic outer world is in part a reflection of the inner world, then it is necessary to know as much as possible of what goes on within. What opposites are at work? What symbols live there? What unconscious forces affect perceptions and influence choices? One of the authors has written on this theme.[39] Throughout this chapter, we hope it is clear that, at the very least, the functioning of the creative ego is required in order that the inner world may be seen with greater clarity and may be chosen with more certainty, and that it is also a way to inner and outer freedom.

Each of these functions of the ego involves choice, perseverance despite pullbacks, and the bringing together of many opposites. These subtle choices made by the "I"—and countless similar choices which make a life—are what determine whether the single continent will be found or not. The answers reside with an essential ego that is, despite strength or weakness, working for what lies beyond its limits. If the continent is to be single, the nation ecstatic, there must be a cooperative relationship with the depths of that interior place of the unconscious from which values emerge. Only if this stage of the journey is taken can man approximate loving God in the Self and in the neighbor with "all."

6

INTO THE MIRROR
OF THE WATERS

*The need and difficulty
of confronting the inner world*

The man who looks into the mirror of the waters does, indeed, see his own face first of all. Whoever goes to himself risks a confrontation with himself.[40]

The look into the mirror of the waters, the encountering of oneself, is a risk? How absurd! I am nearer to myself than to any other! But how much more absurd this second notion is, that I am near to myself. The fact is that this true face is less known to most than any other face he sees. The following dream, of a man who was successful and well adjusted in the outer world and yet was failing dismally in his personal relationships, illustrates how little is known of the inner face.

I am in the central square of a small town. Just as I come out of a store where I have bought something for myself, several black-leather-jacketed hoodlum type fellows come roaring up on motorcycles. One of them hits the store window with a rock, they all grab things from the showcase, start for their motorcycles to take off. I grab the last fellow before he can get away. I demand to see his identity card. Angry and sullen, he pulls out his wallet and hands me his card. I am horrified when I see that the picture on his card is a picture of me. He pulls free and starts to run. I call out, "Come back!"

So it is with many people. Indeed, from a general point of view, so it is with most people. It is precisely the lineaments of our own face that we need to recognize if we are to begin to live a life of love. Because they are unknown to us we fear them. Because we fear them we risk the loss of our unconscious peace if we look at them. Yet this risk is a part of the inner exploration that is necessary as part of the process of knowing "all."

Another example, somewhat more humorous than the above but equally vital to the dreamer's self-insight, was the dream of a woman in the mid-forties, whose overweening pride was in her efficiency. She dreamed:

> I am hurrying to catch a plane to go to an important speaking engagement. I keep losing luggage. I can't get a cab. Finally I am riding a bicycle. I am stopped at an intersection by traffic congestion. I am so angry I want to shout at people to let me through. But I discover I can't speak because a rooster is sitting on my head and his feathers get in my mouth.

What she had to see was her own masculine drive that was not truly efficient, just as the upright young man had to face his evil hoodlum.

Perceptive men throughout history have known about the "mirror of the waters" and have realized that to gaze into it and see oneself as one is was to begin to be, in a religious sense, whole. The process has been described symbolically in many great world myths. Philosophers have talked about it. Religious men have struggled with personal visions found in that mirror and have discovered valid helpers emerging from the dark depths. About four thousand years ago, in Egypt's Middle Kingdom, a dialogue was recorded between an Egyptian man and his Ba, his soul.[41] The man's Ba is opposing the man, who is considering suicide. The Ba is saying, in effect, that he should stop being so concerned with collective standards and goals, and should ask himself what he really wants: "Now listen to me! Behold, it is good when men listen. Follow the beautiful day and forget your sorrow." At last the man sees that the quarrel between himself and his Ba is because he, the man, is unwilling to accept another point of view in himself and has been clinging stubbornly to his usual one. After a further discussion from the man about how difficult life is for him, the man hears his Ba say: "Now give up your complaint, you who belong to me, my brother! You may die of your sorrow or you may again cling to life, whichever you now say. . . . In either case, we shall have a home together!"

It remained for the psychology of the nineteenth century to bring this inner encounter once more to the attention of everyman. There are more than enough good histories of psychology available. It is sufficient to say that since Freud's courageous overturn of the enthroned reason of the Victorian period, words such as "unconscious" ("subconscious"), "complex," "repression," "catharsis," "integration," and a fairly large number of others, are familiar to most educated people.

Although others before Freud (even, let us remember, as far back as Jesus, who said that it was not what went into a man but what came out of him that was the problem) had pointed out that there is much more to a man than what can be seen on the surface, Freud revived this idea in the face of agonizing rejection from his colleagues. The subsurface layer of personality Freud called the "subconscious." On the whole, he believed that this layer was a product of the repression of all contents of infant and childhood experiences which were considered by parents, parent substitutes, and society at large as "bad." Consequently, for Freud, subconscious contents needed to be raised to the surface by finding their childhood sources, and then either eliminated, firmly controlled, or sublimated—"raised" to some better (more acceptable) level of outer expression.

Jung, beginning as a co-worker with Freud, parted with him

—reluctantly—precisely because Jung believed, based on his clinical practice, that there was more to the inner world than Freud had postulated. There was one level of the personality (Freud's "subconscious") based mostly on repressed environmental experiences, and Jung referred to this as the "personal unconscious." But he said that prior to that, prior to all individual experience, was a vast realm of personality which he called the "collective unconscious"—collective because it contained the ancient and usual patterns of behavior common to all mankind. This level of the unconscious is pre-ordered and capable of emergence into consciousness as (1) instinctual patterns of response; (2) creative images and symbolic acts, manifested in ordinary life and in all the arts, as well as in living liturgy; (3) sources of healing due to the psyche's natural order and purposiveness (Jung found the "religious factor" here); and (4) uniting symbols that help to resolve conflicts. All these ways of manifestation of the collective unconscious can be included under what Jung called archetypes, the basic and essential determinants of man's behavior. In the vital matters of why and with what man looks into the mirror of unconscious waters, it makes a great difference whether he approaches it with the attitude that it is a place of terror and destruction, or with the attitude that it is unknown and perhaps terrifying, but has its intrinsic worth and meaningful direction.

To include more and more of an individual's totality is to include the collective unconscious (to be conscious about the experiencing of the archetypes). Jung stressed that there is a natural gradient of the psyche which, if followed and not blocked, will unfold in the direction of fruitfulness of the pre-existent, unique Self. Unfoldment involves energy, a psychic energy that remains constant. This has wide implications for the confrontation with oneself, because if the larger portion of psychic energy is expended in the task of not-looking, there are end products of fatigue, depression, anxiety, irritability, etc. On the other hand, if psychic energy (libido) is permitted to flow in its natural direction, it behaves as any good river or sea behaves, rising and falling with the seasons and tides, making its proper contributions to the interior land and all its teeming life.

We cannot know our inner world directly—in the same way as we can know our heartbeat or our pulse. The actions and reactions of our inward archetypes are known by way of symbols. We "know" through images that stand for something other than, and greater than, themselves. True symbols always have vistas of mystery standing behind them. If they do not, they are signs —as a traffic signal is a sign rather than a symbol.

By our symbols we shall be known. They carry and express our uniqueness and our ordinariness. They impart to life its bright or dark imaginativeness. The artist cannot live without symbols, and sometimes knows it. The child lives unconsciously and spontaneously through them. Most adults live without being aware that they are constantly surrounded by symbols and that therefore their existences are lusterless and often meaningless. If the earth could speak, it might say: "How can I tell man I am here to serve him and be served by him? I will tell him through buds and blossoms in spring, through full fruit at harvest, through winter silences." And if the unconscious world of man could speak, it might say: "How can I tell him I too am here to serve and be served? I will tell him through symbols woven into dreams, myths, religious rituals, art, the play of children, and into all persons or situations or things that move him with joy, grief, fear, anger, despair, love." As soon as we look into the mirror of the waters we are face to face with the multiplicity of our being—best to worst—by way of symbols. And if the "all" is to be used toward a wholeness of living and loving, religiously meaningful life needs to be based on symbolic life made conscious.

This descent into the unconscious inevitably involves an awareness of inner opposites and their interplay. To some degree we all recognize that we have in us those same opposites of good and evil, light and dark, love and hate, fight and flight, gentleness and harshness, that are described in the Genesis Eden myth and in the parable of the Samaritan. A woman who had been brought up in a home where very strict standards of conduct had been imposed upon her and her sister, and who was in turn forcing these same standards upon her children and consequently being estranged from them, went to the theater and saw a play about a prostitute. To her dismay, she found herself identifying with this woman, and was unable to forget her. After losing a night's sleep struggling with her feelings, she said to a friend: "I'm so ashamed! It is terrible to have feelings like this, to feel I might be like that horrible woman!"

This sort of reaction makes the ego become more afraid, and only serves to force it into increasingly rigid, narrow, unimaginative patterns. The creative role for the ego is a dedicated working with whatever comes up, regardless of how painfully opposite it may seem to be to our self-image, and then a bringing into consciousness and an integrating of what is discovered. To deny the movement of inner opposites is essentially irreligious —as it is irreligious to deny the rights and creativity of one or another group of people. And just as society is facing today painful crises of integration, so the individual of our time is facing a crisis of psychological integration of his own parts from which he has been isolated for generations.

What are some of the archetypes (and their opposites) encountered in the mirror of the waters? They are not only the components of the inner world toward which choice must be made but they are also the world from which choice comes. They are a part of man's fate that he can and must incorporate before he can find his destiny. The named archetypes are comparatively few, although their symbolic manifestations in specific individuals and in specific cultures present a bewildering variety. Probably most of what we encounter in our inner journey could be subsumed under the following archetypes (and, in some cases, those complexes in which they most often are involved): Mother or Father (parent images and complexes, not personal parents); Hero (for the woman, related to masculine complexes); Eternal Feminine (for the man, related to feminine complexes); Satan, Devil, Trickster (Shadow complexes);

Child—either as Divine Child (related to Self) or as *Puer Aeternus* or *Puella Aeternae* (infantility of a kind); Mentor (Wise Old Man or Wise Old Woman).[42]

Unless these archetypes are to dominate the psyche, the ego must assume the enormous responsibility for lifting them into the light of consciousness, and for helping to incorporate what is made conscious into the total psychic functioning of the personality. For example, the ego must struggle not to turn away from the negative suffocating aspect of the Mother archetype but must also work to discover and honor that other aspect of the Mother archetype, the maternal nurturance and acceptance. Or, when fear and anxiety come as responses to the judgments of a demanding Father and the archetypal Judge, it is the ego that must hold firm until the adequate standards of discrimination come to light, and the real father can be separated from Father archetypes. And so with the other archetypes. The ego, as center of consciousness, must be the brave examiner of the depths, must neither flinch before nor be inflated about what it sees there, must assume responsibility for the other faces which may appear, and for moving toward their integration and/or transformation.

What do some of these great images represent? The Father archetype is the spirit and giver of direction, meaning, and purpose. The Mother archetype is the primordial container of all substance, the great moving sea of the unconscious, undifferentiated, unknowing and waiting to be known. She *is*. She exists before consciousness begins. Both are bipolar. Together these two "eternal presences"—the Mother and the Father raised to the level of mystery—constitute the deep, numinous, suprapersonal force in whose presence man is aware of his more-than-human qualities, and to which he has often given the name God. Mother-Father God. Both Egyptian and Acoma Indian myths have a primordial Being called "He-She." Some cultures —most particularly our Western contemporary ones—have suffered and still suffer from an overemphasis on the masculine Godhead. It is only through the play of opposites that psychological vitality is maintained. Mother/Father, Eros/Logos, feminine/masculine—these opposites almost more than others must exist in their bipolarity if psychic health is to be found.

The Hero on a journey is a universal archetype of great importance. The adventures of the Hero, the overcoming of obstacles, the achievement of the goal through suffering—these themes have a compelling quality from childhood onward. The Hero is the personification of that courageous and determined part of the psyche which pushes forward despite all hindrances and disappointments. This journey is intimately related to the problem of human freedom. The ego's role is that of continually choosing to follow the Hero rather than trying to escape the challenges of life and turn away. The danger always is that we will identify the ego with the Hero, that we will try to become it instead of serving it.

In the psychological complex known as the Shadow are many dark or only dimly felt archetypes, some destructive and some creative. Satan, Witch, Trickster, Sorcerer, many personifications of the "sins" (Greed, Lust, Sloth, etc.), are faces of the Shadow. At their most accessible, these Shadow figures stand for that in man which he least likes and most heartily tries to cover up. At their deepest levels, they are symbols of total evil. To encounter these shadow beings is particularly difficult because in so doing it is necessary to sacrifice all the idealized self-images so carefully nourished through the years. We must at least assume our humanity and our iniquity and our fallibility.

The Child archetype has two general forms—the Eternal Youth, and the Divine Child. The Eternal Youth is sometimes sexual, sometimes not, but it is always symbolic of the gay, spritely, and irresponsible being who wishes never to be tied down nor to be held accountable. The Divine Child is the archetype of the "new" creature being born out of the coming together of inner opposites, and as such is a universal symbol for the Self. It is well known in pagan, Judaic, and Christian myth, and occurs regularly in contemporary dreams as a human but numinous infant of mystery.

The Self is perhaps the most significant archetype and/or complex in terms of man's full development as individual. This is true because it is both the totality of and the religious center of personality. And insofar as the individual ego is working for wholeness, for individuation, it is working in the service of the Self, which in turn reflects the larger transpersonal Purpose. Although we have already discussed the Self in previous chapters, here a new facet appears. The Self is an archetype and yet with a difference that makes it, so to speak, the most vital of the psychic "organs," the heart that keeps the vital processes moving in a forward direction. It is not only the center of the total personality, but it magnetizes all the opposites into a pattern that evolves in each individual toward wholeness. The evidence that Jung began to gather continues to accumulate, pointing to the facts that this central Self is preexistent in the child at birth as genetic codings, instincts, etc., and that the ego develops from the Self. The Self is lost to sight in infancy or early childhood, and has to be "achieved" again in maturity. When the Self is discovered and touched, or more firmly achieved, the ego then works with the Self as its faithful servant, and knows that it is thereby serving an inner manifestation of the larger Purpose, God. Moreover, the concept of the Self is a moral one, because to live out of the Self is to be centered in such a way that the responsiveness longed for becomes a reality in everyday life.

All these archetypes are seen in symbolic form in dreams, in art, and in many mythic and parabolic forms. One of the extraordinarily comprehensive although brief stories that seems to contain almost all the archetypes mentioned above is the Biblical parable of the "prodigal son." (Luke 15:11–32.) The younger of two sons (the Hero) claims his portion of the inheritance and sets out from home (from the collective familiar and parental traditions). The young man "took his journey into a far country," squandering his inheritance. He eventually becomes a starving swineherd (descent into the underworld, or into the place of the dark Mother, the Shadow, the instinctual and animal world). The young man does all this with great passion and energy, giving himself to each stage of his journey with equal fervor. At last he is spent, alone, hungry, deserted. And "he comes to himself" (felt the urging of the Self), and decides then to return to his father as his father's servant (having gone to the place of the *deus absconditus,* he can now return, for the first time, to the Father). That is, the young man knows at this moment how far the pendulum has swung for him in the direction of his own Shadow, and knows that this must be incorporated into the Father-consciousness. He starts on his journey back. As he nears his home, his father sees him coming and goes out to receive him with love and rejoicing, hears his confession of guilt, and replies by planning a feast because, as he says, "This my son was dead, and is alive again; he was lost, and is found." (The Cry, the total God-Creator, desires wholeness and enfolds the Hero as the Self that has been born through encompassing both the Mother and Shadow opposites. And the universe truly cries aloud in joy when the Self is found.)

These archetypes are also known by seeing them outside of ourselves as projections onto other persons, situations, places. Whatever a man does not know about himself is projected, Jung said. And the knowing of the archetypes comes slowly, much more slowly than does the knowing of most of our projections, so that the whole vast area of the unknown unconscious is projected outside of us first of all. Two thousand years ago a statement was made by Jesus that stands even now as one of the classic descriptions of projection.

> Why do you see the speck that is in your brother's eye, but do not notice the log that is in your own eye? Or how can you say to your brother, "Brother, let me take out the speck that is in your eye," when you yourself do not see the log that is in your own eye? You hypocrite, first take the log out of your own eye, and then you will see clearly to take out the speck that is in your brother's eye. (Luke 6:41–42.)

We see outside of ourselves those things within us which we cannot face—in which case we see our brother's speck and overlook our own log. But we also see outside of ourselves those positive elements which we cannot see in ourselves. This is as great a log-overlooking as the first, except that in the first case the log seems an obstacle and in the second it seems a possibility for building. We do not put outside ourselves only our negative parts. Of course we do do this—particularly in finding our Shadow outside ourselves. But we also project the positive qualities, and when we project our positive elements outside, we tend to see only the negative elements within us. This is one of the bases for the so-called inferiority complex that says: "I'm no good. He (or she or it or they) is wonderful." This other may be husband or wife or friend or some authority figure. It may also be a central religious image such as Christ, or Buddha. And if our own deep positive values are found *only* outside, then we never really relate to them as our own, and so never find our own rich individual experience, nor express our own gifts.

As a part of confronting ourselves, then, the positive *use* of projections needs to be explored. One of the best means of self-discovery is that of uncovering the nature of projections. To project is, of course, as natural as breathing. The danger is to remain unconscious of projections. On the other hand, to become conscious of them is to make ever wider one's own self-awareness.

Adolf Hitler was an objective social evil, and certainly a host of us were legitimately against Hitler and his acts. Yet a surprising number of us had dreams about Hitler as a symbol of a dictator inside us. Through recognizing and accepting this as a projection—despite its outer reality—we were able to understand and deal with a vicious Shadow side of ourselves. The same process can take place in regard to any social attitude involving minority groups, ethnic groups, political groups. It can take place equally in a positive direction with such a figure, say, as Gandhi. Gandhi was in outer fact a great man, living and dying for peace, brotherhood, redemption of the downtrodden. But as dreams about Gandhi illustrate, we need also to find him inside ourselves as a Hero-Self archetype. Through consciously permitting such men to be "mirrors," we deepen and clarify self-perception and the understanding of our own hidden parts. Also, as we recognize our tendency to project in this way, social action becomes much more authentic and creative.

It is our conviction, after long experience, that a major reason why many people turn away from this confrontation with the unknown parts of themselves is that they have no real compass to use through the dark and stormy places of their journey. The prodigal son remembered that there was such a compass in the father, and could move toward (return to) this Other. Here is both the compass and the goal. If a religiously functioning ego can love this Other with all of the Self, then man can risk facing the all of himself. Darknesses, too, are a part of the Self, and the Self is the inner God-image. If a person orients to this God, both immanent and transcendent, as process, he is inevitably forced to look into the mirror of the waters. If the church would also look into this mirror of the ancient waters, from which the living symbols come, it could make once again its liturgies, creeds, and sacraments vital.

7

THE SHADOWS COME

The dilemma of evil

The mirror of the waters reflects to man much that is good which he has never seen in himself. It reflects much that is shadowed and dark and seems threatening. It gives man terrifying views of his real iniquity, of his actual evil, as in the dreams of "good people" cited earlier. Such dreams, and other experiences that individuals have which suddenly show a cruel or tyrannical or masochistic side of themselves, force the knowledge that man is the possessor of evil as well as of good, of iniquity as well as of creativity.

Dante, in the early Hell scenes of the *Divine Comedy,* wrote:

> So I saw the shadows come, uttering wails,
> borne by that strife of winds; whereat I said:
> "Master, who are those people, whom the
> black air thus lashes?" [43]

These wailing shadows lashed by the black air are the dark inner evils that need to be looked at intently and honestly. Only the person who is well on the way, aware of more than a few of the demands and abysses that life holds, aware of his egocentricities and unknown depths—only he can cope with the mystery of iniquity.

Most people on first becoming fully cognizant of their own destructive darkness, cry out, "Who are those people?" They have no idea how terrible the "good" and the "righteous" can be, although the evidence is clear enough. Christian nation against Christian nation in two world wars, a continuing series of devastating smaller wars instigated by Christian as well as Communist nations against less powerful neighbors, the making and using of the atom bomb, the killing of hundreds of thousands of Jews, the raining of flaming napalm bombs on civilian populations—these incredible acts are enough to indict man. Yet each of these acts has been defended as good. Then there is the roster of evils of omission—neglect of natural resources, air and water pollution, population explosion, neglect of poverty areas. All these social ills, and many more, have been chronicled. It is only that we need to remind ourselves repeatedly that these things have their roots in and grow out of the unknown darknesses lying in everyman's unconscious, darknesses that are dark beyond those of all other animals because the light of man's reason and his capacity for self-reflection are bright beyond those of all other animals.

Some of the finest among us harbor evil. A woman who had always tried to think of others and never herself, dreamed of a sinister, dark, and evil creature hiding in her room. A birthright Quaker, upholder of pacifism and the doing of good works, forced two of his children into revolt and antisocial violence because he, the father, had never faced his own inner darknesses. Yet these people, and hundreds of people similar to them, refuse to see themselves as they are, will not acknowledge the evil they do.

Contemporary Western man, inheritor of a dualistic tradition, has tended to see evil as something that he is and ought not to be, that he ought to eliminate by believing in a Christ that would expiate his sins by atoning for him. Some branches of the church continue to put the blame for evil at the door of man's innate depravity. And it is not only religion that has perpetuated this notion. Schools of psychology, sociology, anthropology, have furthered it. Man is envisioned as more bestial than the beasts, and his evil seen as something that can only be contained or drained off but never redeemed. Other animals survive and evolve, or die out, depending upon how well or how poorly they succeed in a flexible and creative interaction with their environment. Man abides under the same laws. Will he, by his stubborn refusal to increase his flexibility and creativity through an inclusion of his interior world's unconscious resources, reach his end as an evolved species? Is it possible that he, like the dinosaurs, may come to an end because of his inflexibility?

If Teilhard de Chardin is right, however, man need not be eliminated as an evolutionary error because he is able to use his high capacity for self-reflection and self-knowledge. He can know his own evil capacities if he will, because he can know his interior being in all its complexities, and by being conscious of his evil he may be able to say with First Man in the Navaho Indian emergence myth: "It is true, my children, I am filled with evil. But I know when to use it and when to withhold it." [44]

What are the origins of evil, the sources of iniquity? Do its roots lie entirely in man? Are they God's punishments? Or is it possible that they reside also in the Godhead? As Jacob Boehme asked, Is evil a part of the freedom in God which, when we choose not to let ourselves be whole instruments, we experience as God's "wrath"?

Those religious influences which have affected many people have been carried through thousands of years of history by the dualistic Persian religion, the teachings of the Essenes, and the post-Jesus teachings of Paul. These influences have tended to split man's psyche into two parts inimical to each other, and therefore also tended to force man into denying one part of himself while affirming the other. Persian (Iranian) thought, based upon the ancient Avesta, or sacred books, sets forth an ethical dualism between Truth and Falsehood and an opposition between Good and Evil. Through Zoroastrianism and Manichaeism, there arose the great opposition between the light, good, mental powers and the dark, bad, material powers. This in turn was also a part of the religious beliefs and practices of the Essenes, who rejected "pleasure as an evil," and who held that the conquest of the passions of the flesh was a highest good, and who wrote about "children of light" and "children of darkness." Paul incorporated many of these earlier ideas—or found them full-blown in his own experiences—and they became part of Christianity. He made much of the idea of original sin. According to Paul, man was contaminated by the guilt of Adam, the first sinner. Man could find redemption from sin only through the light and good Christ, who atoned for man's sins through his expiatory death and his overcoming of Death and Satan. This dualism was contrary to Jesus' thought, as we will point out.

Our heritage from orthodox Jewish tradition, most important where Jesus and his teachings are concerned, although with less effect on later Christianity, has been succinctly outlined by Max Dimont, and a few thoughts from his work will serve as a brief survey of the problem of evil in Judaic religion. In the early Old Testament there is a fascinating sequence running through the creation stories, and through the initial covenants between God and man, in which both God and man seem to struggle with their own wrath, anger, hostility, irritability, longing, compassion, and love. The early Jews established ritual sacrifices—from circumcision to burnt offerings—as a way to placate and please their sometimes erratic Yahweh. Then when the prophets came into the mainstream of Judaism:

> God, they said, did not want rituals; He wanted higher moral standards for men. God abhorred sacrifice, they contended; therefore, it was no sin if one did not offer sacrifices to God. The real sin, they held, was corruption and perversion of justice.[45]

While earlier Judaic ideas of what was evil were on the whole primitive and relatively undifferentiated, there were at the time of Jesus divergent trends in Jewish thought regarding evil. The Pharisees viewed evil as nonmaintenance of prescribed laws and customs, overlooking the inner elements of evil. The great prophets at least pointed toward a more conscious attitude that man himself could take for or against evil, rather than just being evil. This was more adult and implied the possibility of personally grounded morality. Jesus was in this tradition, although his thought and religious teachings went far beyond, reinterpreted, and revolutionized all previous religious imperatives.

Jung wrestled long and unorthodoxly with the problem of evil. The reader is referred to such books as *The Undiscovered Self, Answer to Job, Essays on Contemporary Events.*[46] He also struggled with Christian theologians about the problem. Some of this is recorded in Victor White's *God and the Unconscious.*[47] Father White held that evil is only in man, that it is in fact the absence of good (*privatio boni*) in man and in the world, and that God is the Ultimate Good. Jung maintained that both good and evil are part of man's psyche and also that both are contained in the God-image (Self). The fact that both sides belong to a unity has a profound effect on man's struggle to become whole.

What is important to those who place the primary stress on each individual as a possessor of choice and freedom is that if Jung is even relatively correct about the nature of the psyche, man then becomes a helper of God, a co-creator in a non-Nietzschean sense, to the degree that he understands and learns to cope with his own evil. And if he is a helper as well as a creature, if what he does or does not do to grow in his consciousness (including knowing his evil), acts to further or impede the evolution of life, then he is far more meaningful to himself and far more valuable to the universe than if he is just a recalcitrant and difficult ("fallen") child of a patient Father God.

Once a person is launched on this task of growth, it is as

though the wailing shadows of the Dante poem approach nearer
and nearer, insistent upon being included. Liliane Frey-Rohn
points out:

> At a definite moment of time, the Self seems to "demand"
> that the personality be made complete, *through the recognition
> of what were up until then hostile, immoral, and asocial ten-
> dencies.*[48]

Dr. Frey-Rohn does not say through the *elimination* of, but
through the *recognition* of. Here the Jungian concept echoes
Jesus' thought that it is what comes from within the man rather
than what comes from outside that defiles the man. In other
words, man must know and include these tendencies as part of
the totality of the ego-Self whole. This is an enormous demand,
but essential, as Jesus emphasized. It means the suspension of
all previously held opinions as to what man should be, what
he has tried to be, what he believes others want him to be. It
means therefore the relinquishing of such partialnesses as have
seemed until now to give pleasure and prevent pain.

And regardless of where the origin of evil lies (although what
is seen as evil's source has effects that are not indifferent), once
man considers his evil he is thrust into the very real matters of
sin, guilt, anxiety, resistance, regression, in their double, crea-
tive-destructive aspect. No wonder it seems easier not to deal
with evil!

If we turn back to that momentous period of history which
was at the end of Old Testament chronicles and preceded the beginning of traditional Christianity, we find the Synoptic Gospel
records of the life of Jesus. Jesus, steeped in his Judaic pro-
phetic tradition, was always concerned with man himself as
chooser. Man can decide, Jesus said, whether to be evil or
not, whether to go the way of life or of destruction. These two
ways are there in the nature of things. Man can choose to act
in the direction of one or the other. The backward pull and the
forward thrust are almost equally present and *both exist in the*

divine realm. "Lead us not into temptation, but deliver us from evil." God possessed both capacities, Jesus said. A God who could and would lead into temptation, who could and would deliver man into evil, knew about evil as a God experience. Yahweh planted the tree of the knowledge of good and evil, according to the Genesis myth. Yahweh prayed to himself, as Jewish Midrash tradition says, not to use his wrath, and to let his good overcome his evil. Jesus is very direct about this in the great and simple Lord's Prayer. And man was to become "all-inclusive" as God was, and so to know just and unjust, good and evil, within himself.

In the light of material already presented here, it seems to us that none of the doctrinal religious views of evil encompasses its existential nature as an intrinsic part of personal life and of Life, whereas the thought of Jesus does. And Jung, although he was more concerned with the concepts of the dogmatic Christ and its shortcomings, time and again echoes the ideas of Jesus. We are convinced, after thirty years of work with this material, that by examining the remarkably relevant teachings of Jesus, illumined by modern depth psychology, especially that of Jung, there is a deepening of religious understanding and self-awareness that comes in no other way.

What happens when a person does try to deal with ordinary evil more creatively? Let us take a look at Mr. J. On Tuesday he awakens tired, irritable, closed off from his family, and spends the day trying to escape himself by being egocentric, unaware, and inadequate. He doesn't see what the situation requires from him. He makes erroneous evaluations of himself and of others. He does things that are consciously or unconsciously hurtful, even cruel, both to himself and to others. Failures multiply until at last, exhausted, he falls into bed only to lie awake for the endless hours it takes for him to see what he has done. On Wednesday Mr. J. tries to approach everything with more openness and flexibility. His evaluations are more genuine and sensitive, and he manages to engage in many more dialogues than monologues. In short, by trying to avoid his evil he comes to grief, and by recognizing and assimilating it he acts more creatively and also is more richly fulfilled. As Jesus said, "Whosoever shall seek to wall himself in shall be destroyed, and whosoever shall let the walls fall shall find life."

This "life" includes the mystery of iniquity and the reality of evil. Mr. J. must see, over and over, not only that he can do what is evil, but that he *does* do it. Sometimes he does it through a true ignorance, and only recognizes it as evil after more knowledge is acquired. More often, however, he is evil knowingly. In his hands are his tools and he is quite free to use them for, or against, creative life.

The dream of a young woman struggling with such a condition speaks for itself:

> I was looking down a street and saw a girl lying on the ground, having had a seizure. Nearby were some young men, but instead of helping her they were unconcerned and indifferent. To my horror they started up their car and drove across her body, leaving her there. I was aghast at such behavior, and ran after them, thinking that surely they must be punished.

The farther one goes into depths the more powerful for good or ill these tools become. This woman's dream shows her desire to help versus her indifference, even cruelty, to her feminine needs. Because of such conflicts all the Mr. J.'s of this pressing world resist choosing at the same time that they desire to do so.

Are we all "poor banished children of Eve," as the great "Salve Regina" says? Perhaps so—in the sense that when we embrace the God who is Freedom, we must depart from the God who is parent. The original, undivided but unrealized self —Adam and Eve—had to be plunged into the conflict of Yes/ No in order to be realized as persons, as unique, as having a Self. Eve and Adam decided for conflict rather than for a bland obedience. The garden ended. The journey began.

Banished? Yes. From the fuzzy pleasures of unconsciousness, from infantile, omnipotent passivity, from assurances of just

rewards based on barter. In this sense we are banished. But
in another sense we are launched into free air as baby spiders
are, and we, as they, trail our filaments across the sky until, at
the bidding of patterns of wind and warmth, we find that niche
from which we can begin to grow.

Launched or banished, floating free or dragging back, man,
Adam, Eve, Mr. J., the young woman, are beset by evil and
must find a way to deal with it. Shall it be denied? The smug
and the self-righteous say that it should. Shall it be given in to?
There are increasingly many who say, "Why not? Live it up!"
Shall it be repressed? The tense and the anxious say, "Yes.
People will like you better." Shall it be seen outside, hated,
killed? All the wars of the twentieth century have been scream-
ing that this is the only thing to do.

There is another alternative, stated as an imperative by
Jesus: "Resist not evil." A simple enough injunction, but one
that has been misinterpreted for generations. For not to resist
evil is neither to give in to evil nor to obscure evil. There is
nothing more difficult, nothing requiring a greater courage. It
means that the evil is seen, recognized, admitted—whether
within one's own inner space or out in society. This demands
honesty of a heroic kind, and perception as objective as can be
acquired. And, second, it means that the evil is dealt with
head on.

Whether one is confronted by a dark cruelty in one's own
behavior, or by a bigot with murder in him, it takes courage to
see the evil in the world and yet to walk toward its threat. This
is the heart of authentic nonviolence as a method to deal with
evil. Jesus knew it well. He knew it inside man too. "Be careful
lest the light in you be darkness," he said. (Luke 11:35.) He
knew it as he walked toward Jerusalem. Many others have
learned what he meant. Thoreau, Gandhi and his followers,
Martin Luther King, Medgar Evers, John and Robert Kennedy,
Malcolm X, and the civil rights marchers in the South. They
have known. Socrates knew, holding firm to his inner seeking.
All those artists, mystics, men of science, and unknown journey-

ers who have stayed through their dark and evil hours, who have faced and encompassed both outer opposition and hostile powers, as well as their inner demons—they have known how to "resist not evil."

If a person can be open to doing this, he can cope with the "wailing shadows." He can dare to have "imagination in evil" because he can try creation. He moves a large step nearer authenticity. He also offers to a desperate world the enormous help of one man toward world redemption. And one man, multiplied, could do it.

8

AN OFFERING
AND A RECEIVING

The role of sacrifice

For birth, the neutral comfort of the womb is sacrificed. For growing up, childish things have to be put away. Adam and Eve had to leave Eden in order to be able to return to the tree of life. In order to have a relationship with others, complete personal autonomy has to be given up. For the sake of creating with originality, preconceptions as to the order and composition of things have to be let go. For rebirth in the psychological-religious sense, the hard-won adaptations of the years have to be laid aside. The Samaritan, to be able to express his high degree of compassion, must have already seen his position and reputation torn from him, and he himself made an outcast. How desperately man clings to egocentric defenses, entwined within with projections, and shuns his dark selves, all because he is so reluctant to sacrifice his one-sided picture of himself.

Choice, as it becomes a process of consciousness, inevitably involves sacrifice. There are two kinds of sacrifice—one that is an egocentric although unconscious self-immolation, and one that is a true and willing letting go *to* something man has learned is of larger proportions than that which he lets go. The first is martyrdom. The "dear ego," as Kunkel called it, martyrs itself on the altar of its desire to be praised and loved. This is not true sacrifice. The second kind is a giving up of ego autonomy so that the Cry, both immanent and situational, may be served by the ego. Egocentric self-esteem cannot be maintained if a person is trying to act on the injunction of the two commandments. He cannot love God with all, and his neighbor, and the larger Self in himself, and still hold tight to ego defenses. They must be offered up. In return is offered "eternal life" in the present. The kind of total offering involved in this process of loving becomes the hero deed.

"It is precisely the essence of all sacrifice that it should be at the same time an offering and a receiving," wrote Gerardus van der Leeuw.[49] Man cannot offer up what he does not know as part of himself. He cannot let himself know the deeps and heights of the soul unless he is dedicated to the knowing because he senses he is part of a larger pattern. He has to say Yes! to the desire to serve those processes which lead to the reborn state, to the new man. Then he can undertake the hard work of transformation.

Today, when older religious images (including the traditional God-images) are breaking up everywhere, the question is being asked repeatedly, "What can I be dedicated to?" Some answer: "To nothing but my own personal satisfactions and gratifications. That is all there is." Here man has such alternatives as being "successful," being drugged, and facing alarmingly imminent ecological destruction. Some answer, "To changing society and its ills," making transformation only an outer happening. Still another, "To exploring only my own inner world." But here he will find himself lost in a labyrinth, unable to know the deeps and heights of his own soul unless he has already said Yes! to that Purpose leading to the reborn state of the new man. If he has said this Yes, he is ready for the hard work of cooperating with the inner Hero and thus being transformed.

For example, a young man and a young woman marry, each

believing that the relationship is right and creative. They honor each other, but more as brother and sister, and an emptiness exists that neither recognizes. Aside from occasional quarrels about money or ideas, and momentary doubts and frustrations, their marriage seems to others and to them, good. Then the young man falls in love with another woman—that is to say, he falls from his heretofore secure ledge of adaptation into a sea whose waves toss him about inconsiderately and unreasonably. He does not wish to hurt his wife because he genuinely cares about her. He does not want to lose this new and vital meaning. What is he to do? Shall he set aside the marriage and move into the other relationship? Shall he try to serve both of them at once? Shall he renounce the new and struggle with the old? Shall he work with the new meanings only inside himself? Or only outside? Or neither? Or both? How can he decide what to offer?

If, of course, he is concerned only with being satisfied, he will give up nothing. And in the deepest sense he will receive nothing because there has been no sacrifice. If, however, he is committed to the larger Value and is willing to work at change, then he will hear and heed the Cry as it comes both from the unconscious levels of his being and from his outer situation. In some combination of these he will discover what is the way through for him.

On the other hand, choice and sacrifice thrust themselves into life not only with regard to relationships between a person and an infinite variety of his neighbors, or between him and the transcendent Thou, but also between intrapsychic parts. What is one to do, for example, with a long-buried hostility that has been at last uncovered and faced? Is it to be held on to? Expressed? Let go of? Worked with in some other way? Certainly individual decisions are required, based on inner as well as on outer laws. As one of the authors has pointed out elsewhere, we need to "take the risk to be individuals, finding our own meaning and interpretation." This not only challenges dependence upon outer authority, but also gives "self-respect and a sense of dignity very hard to find in the psyches of those ridden by self-hatred." [50]

Often a dream will show a way to go, and the ego has to decide to follow or not. Following generally brings the ego into a position of sacrifice, because in order to go, the ego must give up its overadaptedness. A very precise, earnest, sometimes humorless man had the following dream:

> I am looking for something unknown to me. I go into a slumlike dwelling, set in a field, to hunt for it. It is bare. No one is there and I cannot find what I am seeking for. I leave but return later. An old crone, dressed in tattered clothes, straggly hair falling down her shoulders, leads me through the house. She is coarse but she has down-to-earth humor and common sense. She takes me to a back room. There, lying on a bed with his back to me, is her husband. I recognize him as the object I have been searching for. I feel very grateful for these humble people who have helped me with my search. They are not sophisticated but have a connection with life and nature.

The ego here went with its own shadowy and uncouth opposite, and by the sacrifice of its own "dignity" found the humble reality it had been seeking.

One essential for a meaningful offering and receiving is the working together of inner and outer purposes—or, rather, the recognition that they do work together. For example, if a man dreams of a hostile enemy, and on the same day has an argument with a friend, he needs to ask himself what the relationship is between these events. Did the dream "cause" the quarrel? Was it only chance? Was something operative both in the inner and in the outer world that could be called purposive? Is there a teleology mirrored from inside to outside, or outside to inside? Does the inner center reflect the universe in such a situation as described above? And vice versa? Is the relationship between the man's dream and his quarrel meaningful? Many people have answered this in the affirmative. Charles Williams referred to such situations as times of "holy luck." Kunkel called them "divine coincidence." Jung wrote at length about them under the term "synchronicity," a principle of meaningful coincidence. All these descriptions imply that, for a sacrifice to issue in a transformation, the ego consciousness needs to tune in on the larger Meaning and see what that Meaning desires to be given.

One of the central teachings of Jesus about the nature of creative Life is contained in a parable:

> The kingdom of heaven is like a merchant in search of fine pearls, who, on finding one pearl of great value, went and sold all that he had and bought it. (Matt. 13:45–46.)

An analysis of this parable, in the context of sacrifice, may serve to illuminate what is meant by this offering and receiving as it takes place within each individual. Jesus again gives the cost as "all." This "all" which is to be sold, unless it is to be taken as martyrdom, needs to be redefined as befits the story. The merchant did in fact receive the best of pearls because he sold everything. What does this mean?

What does the parable require? That I sell my goods (all that I have). Does this mean, as it has been interpreted by much traditional religious teaching, that I give everything to God and throw my ego away? But this is begging the question, is giving up one egocentricity for another; I sell all my pearls and refuse the one. If not these negative actions, what is required, then? My goods must be turned over to the Other, and the "I" then is the steward of the pearl, not its dictator. The egocentric demand to have things as one wants them is sacrificed. The focus from henceforth is carrying out the requirements of the Other (in whatever form one conceives of Him-Her-Thou). Surely the pearl of greatest value is more than what is given up for it. Even so, this selling of all is a heroic task, and certainly sacrificial. As Jung wrote:

> The Self . . . feels our sacrifice as a sacrifice of itself. From that sacrifice we gain ourselves—our Self—for we have only what we give.[51]

After we have given up autonomy, and been "asked" by the real owner to be the steward, it becomes our job to familiarize ourselves with the pearl so that we may use it as creatively as possible. Eventually the ego (I) will perceive that it is at last living with the jewel of the Self, and that it serves the owner (God) by dealing with the jewel creatively and cooperatively. The ego becomes a "Son," a steward for the Holy Spirit.

Is there sacrifice in this painful and difficult process of change of ownership? Yes—in the sense that previous notions of "good" and "bad" management are overturned. More is known; we are therefore responsible for more. Yet out of this sacrifice comes the "pearl of great price." The ego will in its *autonomy* is sacrificed, in order that it may creatively serve the Whole, both immanent and transcendent.

One of the most moving tales of sacrifice and redemption is that of Sir Gawain and the Lady Ragnell.[52] Gawain, one of King Arthur's finest knights of the Round Table, promised, in order to save the life of his beloved king, to marry a "loathly lady" with "a hideous twisted face," "great squinting eyes," one who was enormously greedy and fat and who "sat hunched on her horse like a great bale of straw." Gawain kept his promise, although the entire court was filled with horror. In their bed-chamber on the wedding night, Gawain kissed her, and afterward wept in agony. Ragnell at that instant was freed from enchantment and became her young and beautiful self—but only for half of every twenty-four-hour period. And Gawain must choose, she said. Did he want her beautiful by night and loathsome by day, or the other way around? Gawain answered, "With you is the greatest suffering, and you alone must choose which you are most able to bear." At this final sacrifice, the enchantment was completely lifted and Ragnell and Gawain are freed into loving relationship. Gawain's autonomy of desire had to be utterly and humiliatingly renounced, the natural wish for a lovely wife—all for the sake of the Round Table and its safety. Anguished sacrifices for him! What he had to offer up was enormous. What he received back was more—his king's life preserved, the Round Table secure, and love. He was a servant of the Holy Grail. He found the "pearl of great price" by selling all that he had.

Before leaving the consideration of sacrifice as a way to love God in Self and in neighbor, we will point out some of the pseudo-sacrificial actions that people fall into, and what can be done with them. Many put the conscious side in a ruling position, emphasizing rational "sacrificial" approaches to rational goals. Of course peace is good! Of course minorities should be helped! Of course my husband (wife, friend, children) has the same rights as I! But why can't we be reasonable (my kind of reasonable) about it? It is relatively obvious that unless one-sided conviction of rational rightness is given up, one will get nothing back except platitudes on top with hostility underneath.

That the unconscious not only exists but that it has an enormous amount to say about human behavior is more and more widely admitted. In the same way as discoveries of modern physics have made once stable objects seem shifting and uncertain, discoveries as to the nature of the unconscious have altered ideas about man as a rational animal. One of the dangers inherent in the opening up of this powerful inner world is the danger of becoming identified with separate and unrelated elements of the unconscious. When this occurs man, rendered incapable of choice, is swept by unconscious forces into various forms of destruction.

A final area of pseudo sacrifice lies in the use of inadequately taught or understood Eastern methods of "letting go," methods that, because of basic psychological differences, can easily become retreats from consciousness when practiced by Occidentals. Both Oriental and Occidental religions have, to one degree or another, related morality and sacrifice, and yet the meaning of sacrifice may be quite different. Jung has pointed out many times in his works that there are differences in the psychic structure of Oriental and Occidental man, and therefore that these differences require different psychic directions. The Occidental needs to sacrifice his ego *in its egocentricity,* to be sure, but this does not mean to throw it away, to retreat from consciousness into nothingness. As Occidentals we may need to be open to the unconscious mother-world, as the East has been, but to "lose ourselves" in that world is to give up the best of the self-reflective Greco-Judeo-Christian heritage. As Occidentals, Jung said, we need to experience the absolute necessity of a creatively choosing ego if genuine and lasting movement is to come.

Sacrifice, then, both of ego-centeredness and of egolessness, both of fear and of inflation, is of the very essence of psychological growth and of religious meaning, if genuine and lasting movement toward transformation is to come. Autonomy is offered up. Wholeness is received. An enriched universe is found. Personal gods are sacrificed. The all-inclusive God who is large beyond imagining is rediscovered.

9

MAN'S FRUITS
AS TRADEMARKS

*Nobody else
can be alive for you*

Man can try creation. He can step nearer to his authenticity. Doing this, or not doing this, he is known by his fruits. He shines forth for who he is, or he falls dully into nothingness for who he is not. And although the essence of eternal life is not determined by him, his response to and incarnation of it is.

Possibly these fruits are in part dependent upon the creative visions about them. And the visions are in part dependent upon a man's knowledge and experience of the nature of the wholeness of human personality. If I wait for somebody else to have fruits for me and assume that I do not have the potential of aliveness within myself, my harvest of fruit will be small because I have not expected much. With no vision of aliveness, I have not therefore tended my fields and orchards, have not watered, pruned, plowed, weeded. I have learned nothing about the possibility of abundance. On the other hand, if I have held the vision and undertaken my husbandry with courage, resolved to love with all of the heart, soul, strength, and mind, I will learn the true capacity of my fields because I have explored them. Under these conditions it is likely that I not only will come to know my aliveness but will manifest it in the world.

One of the early and beautiful descriptions of fruitful personality is from The Book of Jeremiah:

> Blessed is the man who trusts in the LORD,
>   whose trust is the LORD.
> He is like a tree planted by water,
>   that sends out its roots by the stream,
> and does not fear when heat comes,
>   for its leaves remain green,
> and is not anxious in the year of drought,
>   for it does not cease to bear fruit.
>   (Jer. 17:7–8.) [53]

A modern poet wrote, in the spare lines poets often use:

> He who was a river into the wilderness
> Is now come back from misery to bless
> The hounding spirit.
> He who was rich and now so seeming poor
> Owns an inheritance which was not his before—
> Even his self.[54]

Erich Neumann, in discussing the mature work of such artists as Rembrandt, Shakespeare, Beethoven, says of these great ones:

> The limitations of the epoch are passed over; they have escaped the prison of time and the ego-bound consciousness. We begin to see that the supreme alchemical transformation of art merely reflects the alchemical transformation of the Great Individual's personality. . . . The creative integration of the personality transcends the contingency of any time-bound form.[55]

He goes on to point out that today, as never before, personality and culture must become more related or both will perish.

Man in relation to himself, man in relation to the absolute, man in relation to others—all these are descriptions of man alive, man having hold of eternal life. Such a man has *personality*. What else does he have? Of what, more specifically, does genuine personality consist? If it is not self-satisfaction, the ability to conform, peace at any price, or what the advertisements label happiness, what is it that man seeks as the fruit of this difficult way?

First of all, and of primary importance for the continuance of risking and becoming, is the realization that there is an interior center, secure and yet flexible, like the nucleus of the cell of personality. Descriptions of this *sense of purposive center* have ranged from "the kingdom of God is within" to T. S. Eliot's "in my beginning is my end, and in my end is my beginning." [56] One of the loveliest and freshest of these descriptions is from a potter:

> We are transformed, not by adopting attitudes toward ourselves but by bringing into center all the elements of our sensations and our thinking and our emotions and our will: all the realities of our bodies and our souls. All the dark void in us of our undiscovered being. All the drive of our hungers, and our fairest and blackest dreams. All, all the elements come into center, into union with all other elements. . . . When we act out of an inner unity, when all of ourselves is present in what we do, then we can be said to be on center.[57]

And Theodosius Dobzhansky, eminent biologist, has written:

> A psychological abyss seems to separate *Homo sapiens* from all other animals. In Teilhard's words, "Admittedly the animal knows. But it cannot know that it knows—this is quite certain." Man is able "no longer merely to know, but to know oneself; no longer merely to know, but know that one knows." [58]

Centered purpose, knowable and become known, is the sacramental sheaf of grain, first reaped at the harvest.

Openness and flexibility follow, for when there is a centered point of stillness there can be much more freedom of response. There is much talk of spontaneity as if it were something that we could possess, could make at will and store away and take out when we wished. But spontaneity, openness, flexibility— these are processes, not things. They can be blocked or set to flowing. If the spring is there and the rubble cleared away, the water will bubble up and out.

Few better examples of this process, with all its simplicity and mystery, can be found than in some of the Zen Buddhist koans (problems that are really answers). Here are two of these, taken from a Zen text:

> A monk told Joshu: "I have just entered the monastery.
> Please teach me."
> Joshu asked: "Have you eaten your rice porridge?"
> The monk replied: "I have eaten."
> Joshu said: "Then you had better wash your bowl."
> At that moment the monk was enlightened.

And this one:

> Ummon asked: "The world is such a wide world, why do you answer a bell and don ceremonial robes?" [59]

One of the great difficulties of the man who feels he is existing in a meaningless universe, and of being therefore constantly on the defensive, is that there is no place to stand and look around and say: "Yes, this is where I am. This is what I am. Here is the other. And there is where we are going." Of course, the more insecure we are the more shrilly we try to say these words and the more discouraging it is to have the words come out as nothing. On the other hand, one of the finest fruits of making the search for "eternal life" is the sense that the words can be said as true. Not as inflexible and fixed and codified words—but as true ones. True as a flowing river is true. We can then *discriminate* between creative and uncreative, between the unloving egocentric demand and the loving all-inclusive demand, between the darkness of fear and the darkness of the Nothing wanting to become Something.

Such creative discrimination is not based upon rules and legalisms but upon that Self-knowledge and Other-knowledge arising out of courageous exploration of unfamiliar continents. From man's inner explorings he makes maps, so to speak. From these maps he can begin to know better where he is going inside, where is up, where down, where is north, where south, where are deserts, where the valleys and rivers in his psyche. Having such a map does not, to be sure, prevent anyone from running into storms, from having breakdowns of equipment, even from getting lost. But having a map can tell a person where to find shelter perhaps, or where there is a town, or a harbor to drop anchor in for the time being.

Tension capacity, the *tolerance of ambiguity, anxiety, and conflict*—these abilities, too, come to man as fruits of the work of becoming. The world in which man lives is, by the very nature of the process of growth, filled with anxieties, conflicts, and ambiguities. Either he expends himself in futile flight from them or in desperate efforts to build a refuge where they are not, or he takes the risk and learns to encompass them in ways that are not resignation, but are creative and new. Let us go one step farther. Let us say that only by the inclusion of the unavoidable conditions which we would rather, from our childish viewpoint, exclude—only by their inclusion (accepting and using them for growth) can man be fully alive. For a man to know "that he was and is in the hand of God" in the anguished midst of conflict, anxiety, ambiguity—this is to be alive in an ultimate way. It is to know joy of the magnitude that can absorb and transform pain.

And joy is a most excellent fruit, one that superbly recompenses for the work. The poet Denise Levertov writes:

> Joy, the, "well . . . *joyfulness* of
> joy"—"many years
> I had not known it," the woman of eighty
> said, "only remembered, till now." [60]

Eternal life, as dealt with by Jesus, was not something to come in a later and other world, nor was it a condition that was removed from the world of men and affairs. It existed *now,* in this moment of time, in love of God, in love of Self, in love of neighbor. It was characterized by relationship rather than by remoteness. It not only changed the man who inherited it, but it spread from him into the environment that surrounded him. This eternal life is far removed from what Buber has called contemporary "existential mistrust." Religious existentialism affirms purposiveness in the universe. Jesus was a religious existentialist through and through—a fact that Christianity has on the whole neglected. Nonetheless, in our time of doubt and distrust and sickness, a number of voices have been raised for the "eternal Now" of the religious existentialist position.

Kazantzakis hammers out imperatives as to man's existential need to manifest Life:

> Gather your strength and listen; the whole heart of man is a single outcry. Lean against your breast to hear it; someone is struggling and shouting within you. . . . This is the moment of greatest crisis. This is the signal for the March to begin. If you do not hear this Cry tearing at your entrails, do not set out. . . . The heart unites whatever the mind separates, pushes on beyond the arena of necessity and transmutes the struggle into love. . . . What is meant by happiness? To live every unhappiness. What is meant by light? To gaze with undimmed eyes on all darknesses. . . . Out of an ocean of nothingness, with fearful struggle, the work of man rises slowly like a small island.[61]

Making aliveness manifest involves relationship to the Other, to make the Other known in the world through individual "existence." It also involves relationship to other persons as persons, not as things.

In such words about matters of "ultimate concern" we are near to the closing of the circle of the two commandments. Eternal life comes by love—love of that Other with everything that a man is, and love of Self within oneself, and of the neighbor. Whether the harvest will consist of the fruits we have been describing in this chapter, or of those darker fruits of self-destruction, depends to a very great extent upon each person and upon the ways in which he works and interacts with Life.

To be fully alive, abundant, fruitful, to be a part of a universe that is evolving through struggle toward more creative individuals-in-relationship—perhaps this is, as Teilhard believed, the future of man. Something "wants" manifestation, must have it, in fact, if self-reflective consciousness can in any way lead man beyond the lower animals. Only man can decide deliberately to have a harvest, and can decide what sort of harvest he wants to try for. All other animals must take what nature gives. Man alone can work with Nature to alter Nature in one of several directions. Thus not only man's fate but also his choice and his will are involved, and his life becomes more than temporal. In the Now, his life can take on eternality.

PART 2

THE WHAT, AND METHOD

10

TO MAINTAIN
HOLY INTERCOURSE

*Today's need for ways
to implement the search for wholeness*

Man has a longing to have Life, Life which comes from the Ground of Being, a longing to feel this Life being born inside himself, to see it in his neighbor, to find it where it could burst forth from the earth. The Way to these longed-for things is not easy, but it is meaningful, rewarding, joyous.

From here on we will be considering how, especially in our difficult and complex world, this Way can be implemented. How can any individual create and maintain in himself and on that small bit of earth he inhabits a "holy intercourse" with all of existence? How can he discover an atmosphere conducive to those freeing attitudes which he is attempting to make central? How can he live so that there are helpful and healing symbols that keep him on the Way?

In a news conference Rollo May, religious existentialist, stated that a decay of the modern age is under way. Our faith in reason and technology has been our only myth, he pointed out, and this myth is dying.

In the golden age of Greece it is almost impossible to find signs of specific anxiety, alienation, lack of orienting values. . . . But Lucretius, writing when the myths were losing their power and attacking them himself, sounds like a commentary on the Great Society. He writes of anxiety, directionlessness and the individual "running away from himself." . . . The same is true for when the medieval and modern myths broke down. Then you had the frantic fear of death, witchcraft, sorcery and, in paintings, the wild surrealism of Bosch. In our day it is LSD, hippies, touch therapy, the boom in psychoanalysis, all sorts of fads and quackery.[62]

What May was pointing to is that the mythic symbols of the depths are not to be found in rationalism and technology. We must find them elsewhere. We can either turn to "all sorts of fads and quackery," or we can go the way of seeking out the Cry—in the self, the neighbor, and the world—and of responding to the Cry with everything we can bring.

Unfortunately, the culture's balance of power seems to be with materialism, self-seeking, hedonism, success, exploitation, technological possibles. The degree to which the power establishment and the church establishment have been synonymous increases the upheavals and desertions. The Christian symbols in their traditional interpretations are no longer adequate because they do not hold the central archetypal values, although the authentic meanings of Christian symbols may be alive in the unconscious. What, for example, meaningfully symbolizes God? Where are there sufficient symbols for the Feminine? Is the Christ a symbol that has any contemporary value? Many ministers, priests, and religions admit to a dearth of meaning in the old symbols, and turn instead to pagan nature forms or to a new social gospel to carry the energy. Regarding the Feminine, Protestantism, on the whole, has ignored Mary. And Roman Catholicism needs to explore why the "black virgins" of the world carry so much power. Women in the church have been only a small and seldom heard minority. Yet it seems to us that unless the feminine principles of nurturance and compassion and joyful love begin to invade both sacred and secular, men and women, inner and outer environments, the power we have generated by way of technological masculine inventiveness will destroy us.

To desire and to work for eternal life, individuals must discover and live in relationship to their own creative masculine and feminine symbols, symbols that speak from, of, and to the deepest elements of life. This requires the best effort of ego consciousness, it requires patience and the taking of enough time, and it requires the knowledge and use of proper techniques. Each person needs to become a laboratory.

The word "laboratory" may be thought of as containing two words: "laboratory," meaning "place of work," and "oratory," meaning "place of prayer." The work to be done is a great work, the magnum opus of the alchemists, the "salvation" of the mystics. And this work is *contra naturam,* against natural inclinations to succumb to the pulls of inertia, collective opinion, unconsciousness. This magnum opus is the redeeming of lost parts, the solving of the riddle of Selfhood, the bringing into actuality of potential joy of life, and the hearing and answering the Cry in the world. It is specifically human. So far as we know the lower levels of life do not have the consciousness for undertaking it.

Perhaps behind all authentic techniques or ways of working lies prayer—but prayer defined as a reaffirmation and self-articulation that orients man to the suprapersonal God both within and without, that keeps him related to those forces which form the context of his life. Without some such framework or attitude (and other words can be used than "prayer," if that word is troublesome), the regressive pulls within man have a good chance of overcoming the progressive thrusts more times than are necessary. We will define prayer as including the whole psyche "given" to the whole Other, whether interiorly as Self or exteriorly as Purpose. Although "transcendent" can mean that which goes beyond and is superior to the ego and its directions, and thus that function which leads man to his goal of

Self, we would extend the meaning. We would hypothesize a *transcendent reality* behind psychic facts (as found in myth, dreams, art) and behind all values in the world (as in every outer movement). We would call the intrapsychic, *immanent,* and the extrapsychic, *situational*—and see both of these as manifestations of the transcendent godhead which is working for and desirous of wholeness in us and our world.

The atmosphere for "holy intercourse," then, needs to be that of a creative laboratory, whether a person is at work or at home, alone or with others, thinking, listening, playing. Moreover, it needs to contain some silence, again no matter where, or what is being done. Neither the laboratory of oneself, nor its silence, must be thought of as constrained or stiff or ascetic in any way. Rather, the sense of laboratory is a sense of alertness and a happy awareness toward everything that comes. The sense of silence is the sense of a space within which new and exciting things can happen that were never heard of before. A person can step into this silence, into this happy place of work and prayer, even in the midst of the turmoil of modern life. If he could not do this, there would be no point in talking about it as the atmosphere of the Way.

There are qualities that can be fostered which will help to keep astir the air in this laboratory and this silence. The presence of the larger Meaning can be called up if certain attitudes and qualities are encouraged. And although it is true that the laboratory and its silence is a part of minute-by-minute activities, it is also true that particular times need to be taken to attend to it. The word "discipline" has fallen out of fashion, as if it were a negative thing, and yet discipline is one of the needful qualities if man is to realize his abundant Self. The setting aside of particular times each day when one can step back from the pressures of work, family, friends, even from the pressure of "having fun"—this setting aside and settling in enables a person to be renewed and restored in a grace-filled pleasure. In these moments—perhaps in the morning before the day begins, perhaps in the evening after the day has ended, perhaps both—he returns consciously to himself as laboratory. He may sit in silence, in "holy uselessness." He may remember who he is and where he is going. He may read a favorite passage from some book or other. He may look ahead, or back, into the day and try to see its directions. He may try to subside into the always present Other. He may take up paints or clay, or enjoy listening to music. Somehow the Presence, the healing center, has been recalled and he has put himself in conscious relation to it.

The qualities of spontaneity, openness, and flexibility are needed so that a person is not bound into sterility even by the necessary bonds of discipline. Although these traits are fruits of the Way they are also developed along the Way. It has been said that if we would look for the unlikeness in things that seem like, and for the likeness in the things that seem unlike, we would more frequently· see freshly. Here is a fresh and joyful seeing, in a dream of a seeking middle-aged woman:

> I saw a tree with roots going down into the cliffs below. The cliffs were gray, lavender, and blue. And there was an ocean below. Then I saw that there were picnic tables around and I got up to speak and said, "And God himself came to enjoy."

The dreamer, who had asked the therapist if she had to believe in God and was told she did not, felt the dream was saying that she should look now to find a new God at work in the earthy and sensuous dimensions of the world.

If man could move into each moment with an alertly cupped but open hand, rather than with a clenched fist or inert and flaccid fingers, he would find larger events even if they were small. One person put it this way:

> I want to want lack, emptiness, *openness*. Relaxation v. tightness, tension empathically with hands clutching, holding fast, and open spreading, cupping not stretching [tense]. Arms: spread, not hugging, huddling. Physical yielding, letting go, from toes up. . . . Bowels of compassion, milk of human

kindness, floating—not erect, upright standing—head back on
water as on a pillow—not stiff-necked generation, not self-
righteousness, rejection, resenting refuge. . . . Waiting, in silence, darkness, to be flooded and floated on the *eternal* tide of
living water. Moved in its direction of love, surrounded and
filled, the same reality inside and outside me. Free.[63]

Someone else might use different words, but the experience is the
experience of openness, flexibility, freedom.

Our subsequent discussion of methods and techniques is based
upon certain empirically derived concepts: that the psyche (personality in its total meaning) is a self-regulating energy system;
that there is within it a polarized relationship between the unconscious and the conscious level; that the symbol (as manifestation of the archetype) is a transformer of psychic energy;
that the I (ego) is essential in the work of transformation; and
that there is in man a purposive movement toward individuation.
To oversimplify this: there is that in man which knows where
it is going, and that can get there if he permits (or works for) a
relationship between unconscious and conscious parts by working with symbols as they are met in everyday life and in dream,
myth, fantasy, etc. In the concrete moment, in daily choices, in
dialogue, in relationships, and in the inner processes, the way
in which the symbol is encountered is essential. And perhaps
the religious crisis can be worked through if, in the place of
the "dead" God, man puts that struggling Purpose which includes darkness and light, feminine and masculine, substance
and spirit, the "within" of man as well as the "without" of
history.

In the following chapters we will be continually discussing
the use of symbols. We will examine them as representatives of
the life of the unconscious—of the irrational world that is as
real as the rational world. We will examine them as projected
outside ourselves. We will talk about how to work with them,
dialogue with them, let them help to deepen awareness and relationship and fulfillment. For the symbol is the language of the
unconscious. The unconscious speaks in pictures, images, non-

verbal forms. The symbol is the "as if" statement of the unconscious. Anything may become a symbol whenever a suprapersonal meaning from the unconscious becomes attached to it. For example, one may be in a reflective mood, sitting under the trees in the country silence. A bird flutters down to hop about nearby. The bird is a bird in all its intrinsic birdness, and may be quite clearly seen in its own right. But if at that moment something else occurs within the psyche of the observer—i.e., the memory of a sudden joyful scene of being in a swing as a child and feeling like flying—that has nothing to do with the bird and yet attaches itself to the bird, the bird becomes a symbol of that something which, as yet, is not fully understood because it was forgotten. The dove of Noah and the dove of Jesus are such symbols, going far beyond their birdness.

And so, with our sense of the necessary recognition of the *labor-atory* with its *silence,* its *discipline,* its *openness* and *free spaces* and its *symbolic contents,* we will explore what can be done there.

II

BECAUSE
OF HIS IMPORTUNITY

*The work of—
and for—consciousness*

Despite the unethical and immoral uses of consciousness (i.e., making and dropping the atom bomb, dumping garbage into space, etc.), it is probably the highest achievement of evolution to date. We need to consider it and its development before we plunge into the unconscious levels of personality. Life's latest acquisition, on this planet at least, is man's consciousness. His personal and his racial childhood and infancy lie below consciousness. Each one of us, concerned with knowing ourselves, begins our knowing where conscious awareness is. Only this ego consciousness can help us to move into our dark and prehistoric depths with at least some chance of survival. We have selected three stories that symbolically illustrate some of the dimensions and functions of consciousness. One is from the Old Testament, one from the parables in the Gospels, and one from a contemporary playwright.

From Genesis comes the story of Jacob and Esau. Jacob, with the help of his mother, Rebekah, tricked his brother, Esau, out of both the birthright and the blessing of their father. Jacob nonetheless became a great leader of his people. And having come for many years on his successful way, he arrived at the borders of the country to which his brother, Esau, had fled. Then he learned that his brother was planning revenge on him for his earlier cruelty. So he sent everything that he had across the river into the land where Esau was.

> And Jacob was left alone; and a man wrestled with him until the breaking of the day. When the man saw that he did not prevail against Jacob, he touched the hollow of his thigh; and Jacob's thigh was put out of joint as he wrestled with him. Then he said, "Let me go, for the day is breaking." But Jacob said, "I will not let you go, unless you bless me." And he said to him, "What is your name?" And he said, "Jacob." Then he said, "Your name shall no more be called Jacob, but Israel [He who strives], for you have striven with God and with men, and have prevailed." (Gen. 32:24–28.)

The second story is a parable told by Jesus immediately after he taught his disciples to pray in answer to their request:

> And he said to them, "Which of you who has a friend will go to him at midnight and say to him, 'Friend, lend me three loaves; for a friend of mine has arrived on a journey, and I have nothing to set before him'; and he will answer from within, 'Do not bother me; the door is now shut, and my children are with me in bed; I cannot get up and give you anything.'? I tell you, though he will not get up and give him anything because he is his friend, yet because of his importunity he will rise and give him whatever he needs." (Luke 11:5–8.)

The crucial words in this parable are, "yet because of his importunity he will rise and give him whatever he needs." One must be willing to demand of God's sleeping side that those needs be fulfilled which come from the soul's hunger.

In T. S. Eliot's play *Family Reunion,* Harry, the hero, has returned home to his family estate, Wishwood, for his mother's birthday. He has married and fled from his home, his wife has

died under mysterious circumstances, and now he comes back
to the center of his terrible conflicts with a sense of being pursued by dark fates, the Eumenides of Greek tragedy. At last,
in a scene with a wise aunt who helps him to look at his problems and see their roots in his own unconscious past, he is able
to confront his fate with new clarity of consciousness. He then
says:

> Everything is true in a different sense,
> A sense that would have seemed meaningless before.
> Everything tends towards reconciliation
> As the stone falls, as the tree falls. . . .
> . . . .
> Why I have this election
> I do not understand. It must have been preparing always,
> And I see it was what I always wanted. Strength demanded
> That seems too much, is just strength enough given.
> I must follow the bright angels.[64]

Each of these stories tells of deep needs—for blessing, for
bread, for respite from anxiety and fear. Each of them tells of
the use of patience, importunity, an enduring of the terror and
the darkness and the aloneness. And in each of them someone—
Jacob, or the man with no bread to give his friend, or Harry
—has to stay faithful to the need, confront the unknown power,
receive from it the necessary exchange before life can go forward in fullness.

If we take these persons as symbols of things within the individual psyche, as archetypal images, and look for the Jacob
within, the Harry within, the inner one who has the empty cup-
board—we are already beginning to use a technique for growth.
With whom (in a story, parable, play) do I identify? Can I be
concrete about the ways in which this inner figure could behave
differently toward problems and needs? What kind of consciousness is represented by the different characters? Do I have this
kind of consciousness? Where might it be found? How used?
These and many other questions can be asked of such material.

If one is honest, and in earnest, it is likely that he will find more answers than he would have supposed.

Jacob *knows* that there is something to be met. He meets it, at night, without encumbrances, and stays with it through pain and long struggle until the blessing comes to him. The man who has no bread for his friend *knows* where it can be found, goes to the place, and keeps pounding on the door until he receives it. Harry stays fighting within the misery of the parental complex, lashing out at his tormentors but never turning his back on them, persistently trying to understand more and more about himself. At the end he is ready to follow instead of to feel pursued. These various stories reveal that although the inner Self knows where healing resides, it is the conscious thrust (the ego) which acquires the knowledge and acts for the Self out of that knowledge. Unless the man in the parable had knocked at the door again and again, the holder of the bread would not have given it. Unless Jacob had refused to let go, he would not have received his blessing. Unless Harry had consciously faced his fate, it would not have been finally seen as "bright angels."

In each of these stories there are several major aspects of consciousness clearly shown. First of all, there is *devotion* to the following of the Way. Jacob knew where he wanted to go, knew where his dark brother was, and knew he had to go alone to meet him. So also with the man seeking bread for his friend, and so also with Harry—each of these had a sense of direction and meaning which kept him on the journey. It is well that a man finds these in himself, because only prior commitment to a path will keep him on that path.

A woman who had worked intensely and devotedly at uncovering the inner blackness that filled her dreamed:

> I was in a house, on the second floor. All the windows and doors were open, and in the semi-darkness I could see a shadowy figure approaching, very sinister and threatening; I waited where I was for him to come. I was frightened but aware I must meet him. I tried to call for Bill, but no sound came from my throat,

as hard as I tried. The figure kept approaching. Finally it was upon me and I decided it was no use to call Bill's name. I called "Life." This time the sound came and I awoke.

Because she was dedicated to Life rather than to her ego or any of its goals, she could face the sinister figure with courage, and could also relinquish her demands on Bill and call for the force of Life. A first concrete step for anyone can be dedication to the exciting search for this force. Very few, if any, slide into wholeness!

A second necessary attribute of consciousness is *perseverance*. To the degree that one is egocentric he is easily dissuaded from the work of growth. To the degree that he has struggled to free himself from egocentricity he is able to stay with whatever must be stayed with to persevere until it has been transformed. In the parable on importunity, Jesus is really saying that prayer requires perseverance because there is an aspect of Purpose that is asleep and must be wakened by knocking and demanding. When the man perseveres, the holder of bread arises and gives in abundance. As inner drama, this parable would be something like this: At some dark time, a hungry part of the psyche makes itself and its needs known to consciousness. The ego recognizes that there is a needy party. The ego also knows that it does not itself have the necessary nourishment for the hungry "friend." But it is the ego that has the insight, the devotion, and the perseverance to keep on to where nourishment is. One young man, desperately seeking some meaning for his existence, cried out: "I don't know who I am! There's something that knows, somewhere, and I've got to find it! I'm going to find it! But, my God, it's hard!" Another example is that of a woman who had been beset by a series of inner and outer "bad luck" events—but she worked with them courageously day after day. "They have meaning," she said to a friend. "If I stay with them, I will know."

Discipline also is essential to Life-finding. Discipline can be defined as the regular use of techniques to keep the ego creatively related and obedient to total commitment to Life as a given. Old habit patterns are deep and hard to change, and yet there must be a fundamental reorientation of all old patterns if a person is to be whole. To have discipline is perhaps to ask, in some way, each day, "What is the message of the bright angels that my ego must hear and follow?" And once heard, it demands to be acted on. In this sense, to be obedient to the soul's deepest wisdom is to be disciplined in the way that an athlete is disciplined. Man will spend hours each day practicing some athletic or artistic skill, but assumes that a flabby and uncoordinated ego is capable of making crucial choices for him. A dream shows how the ego can be seduced away from its dedicated work for consciousness, and how also it can choose not to be seduced.

> I was waiting for my analyst. I was in deep meditation. It was in a garden. Finally she came with a friend to dig up one of the plants to send to someone. Then the analyst started upstairs, and I followed, as I was to see her. I was aware of the sort of dancing movements I was making as I went. A man passed me and pulled me. He was boisterous, rough and insensitive. I was now alone with him. He was very strong. I pleaded and screamed and fought with him, and he overpowered me. I felt I could not get away. Then I saw my chance. I pushed him away enough to strike at his groin. I tempered my blow so that I would just touch his clothes and not really hurt him. This shocked him so much, when he realized the implications of my action, that he was speechless. I said to him, "It is too bad that I have to go to such extremes to make you understand that I must go on up to my therapy." I smoothed my clothes and then went on upstairs.

The dreamer, whose problems were not fundamentally sexual ones, correctly read this as a statement warning her to be disciplined—which was hard for her—if she was to be whole. The authentic mystics, men and women, worked rigorously for transformation, expending as much energy to improve as any athlete, finding as much joy in the results of their work as any creative artist. God, and the finding and serving of God, in the world and in themselves, was their total concern and happiness. As Juliana of Norwich put it, she learned to be "buxom and supple toward God." [65]

If the ultimate concern is for the Cry and what it needs if it is to be fulfilled, then consciousness must be strong enough to act. This means daily choices, the taking of certain times for re-collection, discipline, perseverance. This is not an ought kind of work energized by some parental or other authority problem. If there is ultimate concern for Life, then faithfulness, goal-directedness, ego commitment, and obedience will be toward that Life. And the attitudes developed in consciousness and oriented toward that Life will increase its abundance.

12

FOR EVERYTHING THERE IS A TIME

The need for risk and creative disobedience

In the book of Ecclesiastes it is written:

> For everything there is a season, and a time for every matter under heaven: . . .
> a time to plant, and a time to pluck up what is planted; . . .
> a time to cast away stones, and a time to gather stones together; . . .
> a time to seek, and a time to lose;
> a time to keep, and a time to cast away.
>
> (Eccl. 3:1–2, 5–6.)

If man is to be able to be obedient, he needs time to work at it, and more often than not to have time involves some sort of disobedience. Who says when to plant and when to pluck up? How can the time to cast away and the time to gather together be separated? What is the time to keep, as different from the time to cast away? Are these choices based upon just what a person wants to do? Are they based upon what he thinks he *ought* to do? Are want and ought to be joined so as to please everybody? Is it better to say "I won't," just on principle? Or is there some quite other basis for decision? (It could be helpful, incidentally, for the reader to try to answer these questions for himself before going farther.)

Risk, obedience or disobedience, and knowing which is appropriate: for the writer of Ecclesiastes, there were times for each, and each was to be honored. Time and choice were partners. Not so in our stepped-up, hectic, machine culture, where most of us deal with time by rushing from one thing to another until we are exhausted and then fall helplessly into some form of inertia and time-wasting. Increasing numbers of people—and of the older as well as of the younger generations—are dealing with time by dropping out of it with the aid of drugs or television into the timeless world of the unconscious or the trite world of the nonconscious, with no ego direction or concern. Neither the man who rushes about "doing things" nor the one who escapes by alcohol, drugs, or television is getting the total psyche involved in Life. They are not taking the risk of coming consciously to the hidden, inner resources. The rusher says, "I don't have anything to offer," or, "There is too much to do to take time for myself." The dropout says, "The world doesn't want what I have," or "It's more fun just to enjoy."

But it seems to be that only if man consciously uses what he has, can he find himself and the Other. This takes time. It also involves risk, because to use consciously what he has and what he finds as he goes along in the paths of self-discovery means that he will inevitably blunder. People may laugh at that side of him which is most poorly developed. To face this is to risk the loss of false self-images. The unforgettable Greek, Zorba, challenges his overintellectual and unhappy boss in these words:

> No, you're not free. . . . The string you're tied to is perhaps longer than other people's. That's all. You're on a long piece of string, boss; you come and go, and think you're free, but you never cut the string in two. And when people don't cut that string. . . .[66]

Stealing time is a major way to practice creative disobedience and thus to participate in some of Zorba's "folly." Where is this time? Is there ever enough time in the world? Time is stuffed full with role-playing. But if a man steals back time from the ways he usually spends it, if he risks cutting the string, if he goes against the oughts and toward the needs of his psyche, although he is being disobedient to partial needs, he is being obedient to the Whole.

Suppose that instead of always saying Yes to everyone who asks you to do something—a Yes that has come all too often from the desire to be thought well of—you say, "I'm sorry I can't make it," or, "I have a date" (which may be with yourself). Suppose that you set aside a half hour every morning, regardless of what other things seem to be more urgent or more important, and use that half hour just to sit and reflect. It takes a great change in attitude to be quiet, to be relaxed, in the midst of a rushed life to descend into the mystery of oneself. Even little thefts of time are helpful, midstream of a busy day, just to turn from tension, anxiety, hurry, into a quiet place where we can remember once more where we are going.

Many myths portray disobediences of various kinds in the heroic journey. Prometheus, the ancient Greek Titan demigod, disobeyed the command of Zeus and stole fire from Olympus (or from another Titan) in order to bring it to man. For this theft he was cruelly punished by Zeus. Because of his concern for mankind, he risked, he disobeyed the ruling power, and thus mankind reached a new level of culture and consciousness. Who is this disobedient Prometheus in the psyche who goes against the father-authority and gives new light? How can man let him (even help him to) act with his intensive thrust in man's behalf?

In the Old Testament myth, Jacob disobeyed the tradition of the fathers and stole from his brother, Esau. Yet in this deception and disobedience he was supported—indeed, was urged on —by Rebekah, his mother. And in the end it was Jacob who received a second blessing and a new name: Israel, the leader of his people. Jacob was, as was Prometheus, wounded in the bringing of a higher level of consciousness. Jacob, similarly to Prometheus, deceived and disobeyed the father-authority. What would it mean inwardly for the second-born (younger, thus inferior) part of us to go against usual ways in order to be blessed? How can we thus choose the "time to pluck up what is planted"?

A third mythic situation of creative risk and disobedience involves a youthful hero of Navaho Indian legend. Natenesthani (He-Who-Teaches-Himself) [67] is, as Jacob was, the youngest and thus less important child. Having gambled away most of his family's possessions, he is threatened with punishment and possible death, and is driven out. He decides he will go alone on the long journey to the end of the River of Life, is told by the gods that he cannot make it alone, but that they will help him when he brings them sacred beads, buckskin, and medicine. These he steals from his family. Nonetheless he is taken through the entire journey by the gods with no condemnation from them for his stealing, and at last becomes the divine bringer of a new Chant. "A time to seek, and a time to lose" would seem to belong to the story of Natenesthani. How can he be recognized? Where can he be found? Who is this young rejected part in man which must wrest from the old ruling family the values to be used for growth?

If, in all these stories, the question is asked as to what had to be risked, inwardly or outwardly, it was the entrenched behaviors, the collective values, the customary roles. These do not wish to be deposed, resist the coming up of newer and younger and fresher attitudes. Creative disobedience comes, as we have seen from myth and drama, when the new growth point pushes itself against the established order, against the "old gods" (family, tribal head, Zeus, or the dark and stubborn side of the God-image). The cost of thus risking is possible loss, loneliness, wounds, estrangements, even death. The breaking of old patterns is always hard and man's resistance great. But the rewards are greater.

These dangers and their creative outcomes are shown in dreams as well as in myth. A man who had spent many years being destructively obedient to the father images and the oughts in the environment around him dreamed this:

> I am traveling up a difficult mountainside. As I near the pass, I realize that the Pope of Darkness reigns here, and that the only way I can go on to find the valley I seek is to disobey him. I head for the pass, determined to do so.

And an impressive outcome of confronting the binding rules and risking much by breaking them is shown in the dream of a woman whose mother had penalized all her own and thus her daughter's instinctive responses and had led the daughter to obey the same rules:

> Somebody has tied a small black cat to a building, has put rocks in its mouth, wooden blocks on its feet, and has tied a homemade bomb around its neck. If the cat moves, the bomb will blow it up. When it sees me, its eyes are wild with hope. I get behind it, carefully untie the bomb, free the feet, then turn it around. All the tension leaves its body, its expression is one of joy, and it has become softly black and white. I open its mouth to be sure all the rocks are gone—and inside its exquisite pink mouth is a tiny and benign dragon that I know belongs.

By disobeying the old restrictions, and taking a real risk for newness thereby, her instincts were set free, even protected by a diminutive and delightful dragon, totally opposite to the dragon of "don't."

When is the time to throw away stones? When is the time to gather? When is the time to keep, and when the time to cast away? When is the season? "Blessed are you," says the noncanonical statement, "if you know what you are doing." But how can a person know? By taking the time to learn the time. By wanting the fire, as did Prometheus, or the blessing, as did

Jacob, or the journey of Life's river, as did Natenesthani. By being willing to risk and disobey in order to achieve these things. When is it time to act? When is it time to sit and incubate? When is it time to plant? To pick? Planting involves the deliberate and conscious work of the ego to put new meanings into the psyche. Picking involves the finding and using of what is beautifully there for new purposes. So there is effort. And waiting. Risking. Disobeying. And being. And peace of mind. All these add up to becoming. And all becoming means that there must be time to become.

13

SWELL WITH PRIDE
AND VANITY

The need to see our
egocentricities in concrete ways

Why is it not possible to move forward directly, once there is the desire to be whole? Almost three centuries ago an English mystic told it this way:

> How many people swell with pride and vanity, for such things as they would not know how to value at all, but that they are admired in the World? . . . How fearful are many people of having their houses poorly furnished, or themselves meanly clothed, for this only reason, lest the world should make no account of them, and place them amongst the low and mean people?
>
> How often would a man have yielded to the haughtiness and ill-nature of others, and shewn a submissive temper, but that he dares not pass for such a poor-spirited man in the opinion of the world? Many a man would often drop a resentment, and forgive an affront, but that he is afraid if he should, the world would not forgive him. . . . But as great as the power of the world is, it is all built upon a blind obedience, and we need only open our eyes, to get quit of its power.[68]

To be sure, this opening of the eyes is not so easy as William Law makes it sound. It is, however, possible.

These walls of pride and vanity need to be dealt with early because they stand solidly in the way of realizing the Self. Although they are irritatingly difficult to admit to—because man does not like to see himself as he really is—yet they are too high to be ignored. Unless they are faced and pulled down, these walls of pride and vanity will forever be between man and his wholeness. Whether his pride is the kind that assumes he can do everything, or the reverse kind that assumes he can do nothing, it is an attitude far from the real ego, and far from being any help for either an inner or an outer totality. There is something to open our eyes to. Yet first there are things that must be removed. These are the self-images built up from infancy onward, which act as protections against the difficulties of the real world. They are held on to with fierce possessiveness despite the fact that they have no value for real survival.

Such anxieties, pretenses, and defenses have their origins in what is done to man's growing ego in childhood. During those years parents, teachers, society, set forth certain behaviors that are rewarded and certain behaviors that are penalized. A child soon learns, quite unconsciously, what behaviors will secure "love" or approval, or at least safety, and what behaviors will not. These ways of behaving become internalized and entrenched by adulthood. The following dreams, of a young man in his twenties, show how his ego had learned self-indulgence and a sense of being extraordinary to protect him from the demands of the family and from self-discipline. The first dream:

> We take care of the needs of the body 100 percent, but of the needs of the spirit, nothing.

Then a few days later came this dream:

> A voice said, "Must we try to be big things, or must we try to be persons?"

And the same night:

> I see a man and woman, spies, murdering a young woman. I
> don't tell police although they are nearby. Then a man I know
> is shooting at others. Police get him. I say that I'm not a
> policeman.

The dreamer felt that police were "plain and ordinary, but
helpful," and said that he was still avoiding being this. His
built-in defenses (learned in a loveless childhood from gifted
but neurotic parents whose own defenses cut them off from
ordinary family concerns) were to put his bodily needs (especially the erotic ones) ahead of any others, and to be "extraordinary" at all costs. His simple feelings were being killed as a
result.

At an opposite pole was the woman who had learned to get
security by never putting herself first, by always "thinking of
others." A turning-point dream for her was this:

> I am trying to get dinner for all my family and friends. As I'm
> trying to prepare, I drop the roast. Then I find the lettuce is
> spoiled, and there are ants in the cake. "Nobody cares what
> happens!" I cry.

The truth was that, in trying to please everyone by her selfless-
ness, she herself was not caring what happened to her as a
whole person.

Fritz Kunkel gave many graphic descriptions of the states of
mind that result from the successful or unsuccessful attempts to
keep such defenses intact.[69] Whenever such attempts get the
love, approval, or safety desired, the person feels "plus one
hundred"—on top of things, riding the crest. Whenever the
attempts do not produce the desired results, the person falls
down to "minus one hundred"—is in the abyss, in the trough
of the wave. To begin to deal with egocentric defenses—as a
step toward uncovering the real person—is to learn to know
something about the swings of $+100$ moods and -100 moods.

One needs to recognize their existence as moods; one then needs to ask what kinds of situations produce each swing of mood. Such situations can be traced back until the person can see what kind of egocentric image lies behind the mood. Only after taking such steps as these can defenses be let go and a move made toward more creative ground. It is well to remember that, as Kunkel emphasized, it is facing the −100 moods that most often helps us to be the real person we could be. Usually −100 is closer to the real Self because creativity generally is in repressed realms.

There is a Pueblo Indian folktale [70] about Coyote that shows what happens if these egocentric moods are not faced. Coyote leaves home because his babies are peevish and he is irritated. He meets Locust sitting beside the path, making her pots and singing a song. Believing her song will help him with his babies, he demands it of her. Because he threatens to kill her, Locust reluctantly teaches him and he starts home. But he forgets the song when some ducks scare him. He returns to get the song again. Locust, seeing him coming, sheds her skin, fills it with sand and leaves it beside the pots, then hides in a tree. Coyote once more demands, then threatens, then in anger eats her sand-filled skin. When he realizes, upon returning home, that he doesn't know the song, and believes he has even destroyed the singer, he dies when he tries to cut himself open to take Locust out. Poor Coyote here is a tragic-comic everyman, the victim of egocentric demands so narrow that he is unable to soothe his children, sees the gentle potter as something to be exploited, and never finds his own song. If Coyote could have seen into his moods and followed his insights with an honest facing of himself, his life could have been filled with his own song.

Another wryly humorous episode from myth is the story told of the great Algonquin culture hero, Glooscap,[71] who boasted that there was nothing and no one he could not subdue. A woman questioned this, and smilingly pointed to a baby sitting on the floor playing. Glooscap commanded the baby to come to him, and whistled but got no response. Glooscap raged and threatened, but the baby only howled. Glooscap called up all of his powerful magic. The baby looked bored. So Glooscap fled in defeat, while the baby said, "Goo, goo."

The individual can begin to do what neither Coyote nor Glooscap did, by considering those situations in which he feels most +100, on top of things, approved, safe. Then he can examine those situations in which he feels most —100, downtrodden, unloved, disapproved, insecure. For example, John Q. found that his +100 moods came when he won at golf, or was the life of the party, or outwitted a competitor in business. When he lost a golf game, or no one laughed at his party antics, or a business deal failed to come out the way he planned, he was plunged into a —100 mood. He began to see that behind his +100 was a terrible desire to "shine forth" and so to be approved. Behind his —100 was the terrible fear that he wouldn't be approved, that he might fail. As he moved back into his childhood, he began to recall how many times his father had said to him: "Come on, Johnny boy! You can do it! Don't let anybody get the better of you!" Of course, for John Q. to face his —100 moods, to "let go" of trying to win, to accept the fact that a genuine person sometimes does a good job and sometimes doesn't, took all that he had of courage and of real devotion to the journey.

This sort of facing up to the —100 situation is what Kunkel called the "crisis." One must live through a confrontation that he feels he would rather die than do. Only then can he see that not only does he not die but that great energy is released for creative use. A young woman who was painfully sensitive about anything that might cause her to be laughed at, and was strugling to overcome this, had the following dream:

> I left an apartment building and started across a street. It had been raining and the street was very muddy. Right in the middle of the street I slipped and fell flat in the mud. I sat up, a real mess, and looked around. Had anyone seen me? Horrified, I saw that on both sides of the street windows of apartments

were open and people I knew and people I didn't know were looking down at me and laughing. Before I could decide what to do I began to laugh too.

She said that she wakened feeling happy, and that day she was able for the first time to come through an outer —100 situation in the office without the agonizing self-hate that ordinarily would have paralyzed her. She not only lived through it, but found a new respect for herself and a better relationship to her employer and co-workers.

Another and very different example is that of Jane Z., a woman in her middle years. She thought of herself as strong, as being able to face any difficulty and move ahead, as not being one of those people who gave in to things. But a sickness of body made a sickness of soul, and she was besieged by grief, sadness, fatigue. To face these feelings was her —100 situation. She began to see, in facing them, that in her childhood her sister had always been weak and dependent and that her mother had disliked this sister. So she had learned that independence and unfeelingness got approval. Now she had to unlearn.

Why is it that seeing these —100 moods and facing them is not easy? Because it means giving up life patterns by which one has gained false security. But if a person begins to list them and then analyze them with as much honesty as possible, he will find that positive energy is available—energy that has been tied up for years in maintaining the defensive stance. On the side closest to his feelings, instincts, and impulses, man has learned to be dishonest, and to employ egocentric defenses to maintain this dishonesty. He pretends to feel what he does not feel; he pretends he doesn't feel what in fact he does. The result is that very often he no longer knows what he feels about anything. For many people a first step in getting rid of egocentric patterns is to begin to try to find out where their feelings are, and what they are, and where they might lead if they were acknowledged and expressed.

There is no need to proliferate examples of ego-centered behavior here. We refer the reader to such writers as Kunkel, Alfred Adler, Karen Horney, for their rich discussions of types of defenses and methods of working at them. A good summary of many of these can be found also in *The Choice Is Always Ours.*

No man will have it said of him, as a poet said: "Behold, he has done one thing well. He knows whereof he speaks, he means what he has said, and we may trust him," [72] until that man has overcome his "pride and vanity," has dealt with his Coyote, his Glooscap, has worked through his —100 to his reality. Egocentric defenses stand between man and the ability to reach his own reality and his capacity to love God, the Self, and his neighbor. He has to choose to see his defenses, to get at their origins, to work at eliminating them. Facing the abysses of loss of ego defenses is a heroic and exciting task.

14

WHAT DEEPS
GO UNPLUMBED?

*Resistances, distractions,
and regressions to be met*

As soon as man begins to uncover egocentric patterns and tries to deal with them, he uncovers also whole armies of inner enemies that arise to fight against his efforts. That part of him desiring newness is almost overcome, time and again, by those parts of him holding to the old, wanting things to remain as they are—sterile and deceptively secure. These sorts of battles the mystics called times of "purgation." [73]

A modern poet, in a dialogue between God and a man, puts it this way:

> *Do you think, O man, in that high*
> *Toss of desire, that sheer*
> *Aspirative hanker of yours,*
> *What deeps go unplumbed?*
> *Something within you is grinding its axle,*
> *Spitting out sparks.*
> . . . .
> Fingered down in my deeps, I deny it.

What desolation, that Depth!
Who says so!
What secret, that scrivening!
My own business, you.
Leave me alone.[74]

What man denies in his "aspirative hanker" after wholeness is that the unplumbed depths beneath his desire are "spitting out sparks." And he wants to turn away, telling God to leave him alone. Thus the first response to what is uncovered, once some of the defenses are removed, is *resistance*. When defenses are collapsing, the old ways of response lose their efficacy. All manner of things, long since forgotten and repressed, rush in. Our balance is threatened. We fight to retain it. This is resistance. It is not altogether negative because often it forces us to go at the only pace we can safely go and not lose our identity. But it is not positive because it continually throws up smoke screens that keep us from seeing the newness which is in fact at hand. A young woman who, with all her strength, was resisting the insight that life might have value, told the following dream:

I'm in a windowless little cell. On the wall in front of me a hole appears, letting a shaft of sun in. The hole gets bigger. Someone is opening up my cell by removing stones from this wall. I take some cement and begin putting the stones back.

Along with resistance often comes *regression*—the falling back into childish responses of fear, anger, spitefulness, retaliatory actions, withdrawal, and the like. Regression has a factor of choice. Man has always the possibility of choosing for evil (partialness and defensiveness) rather than for good (wholeness and purposiveness). He can let himself fall into the arms of his shadow and until-now denied negativities, cruelties, insensitivities, stupidities, etc.

All sorts of *distractions* come in along the way to further resistance and regression. They are not hard to recognize. They are those uninvited and seemingly intrusive elements which break into the serious work a person is trying to do and sends him off on wild-goose chases and makes him forget where he was going in the first place. They also make an individual discouraged, feeling that he is getting worse, not better. Our experience is that all of these—resistances, regressions, and distractions—contain positive meanings behind the negative effects, although the positive meanings can only be known after a person has followed the negative to its depth.

There are ways a person can work alone. One method available to anyone is to keep a notebook in which he writes down, during times he has kept for himself, answers to (or at least struggles with) such questions as:

What are the excuses I give myself, or hear from others, for not working at this journey? ("I can't do it well enough." "There isn't time." "People will think I'm crazy." "I keep having headaches.") Each has his own sort of excuse. For every excuse, try to see what would happen if it were faced and worked through.

What sorts of people bother me the most, and keep me from concentrating? (Whining people, argumentative people, noisy people, strong people, weak people, and so on and on.) Try to discover whether these may be qualities inside yourself that must be acknowledged before they can be harnessed creatively. They may have come from childhood experiences with parents and siblings, experiences never resolved.

When I am thrown into a —100 mood because of the shattering of an image, what is my first response? ("I never have any luck!" "Why don't people leave me alone?" "I'll show them next time!" "She just doesn't have any sense of humor.") But is man's life merely a series of events, lucky and unlucky, meaningful and meaningless, strung together from birth to death? Perhaps my life is something different, something in which I have in fact participated as I move in the direction of a goal not always known, but there. What would I learn if I would stop from time to time and ask myself the question that the Lord God asked Adam—"Where are you?" To write the answers to this question as a kind of personal history can bring unexpected healing.

Another way of working at resistances and regressions is to write as graphic a description as possible of (1) what kind of a person my parents wanted me to be, (2) what kind of a person I believe I am, and (3) what kind of a person would be the opposite of (1) or (2). Comparisons of (2) with (3) can give further clues about self-images and other-images, with (3) very often holding the key to patterns of resistance and regression because it describes what threatens. For example, a man who had always been in full and rational control of himself thoroughly disliked people who cried. His parents had always rewarded unemotional objectivity. At the time of the funeral of the assassinated President John F. Kennedy, he wept uncontrollably. Persons (1) and (2) in him were engulfed by person (3)—with the result that eventually the man began to honor and to utilize his buried feelings.

Try to list which of the following you use to "escape from freedom": altruism; pseudo generosity; doing good for others, but with, hidden behind it, hostility and self-pity; busy-ness; pressures from outside and clamor from inside; sense of worthlessness, "little-old-me-ness"; independence that is arrogance; attachment to physical symptoms. If you are willing to look at some of these escape devices and with some embarrassment acknowledge them, you have taken one more step toward essential reality.

When man comes to the matter of distractions, he needs to recognize that they are basically expressions of regression and/or resistance—that is to say, he uses distracting things unconsciously to justify regressive and resistant responses. He says: "Well, I couldn't collect myself today. People kept telephoning and asking me to do things." Or he says, "If it weren't for those noisy neighbors, I might be able to write in my journal." In both cases he wants to be distracted. At the same time, there are distractions that contain in themselves potentials for healing. For example, a man who has been working intensely to

master a certain technique of meditation was continually being
distracted by the image of a clown dancing. As soon as he
followed the distraction rather than the meditation, he was led
toward a long-buried and much-needed sense of humor. So
there is a critical problem of discrimination involved. When
should a distraction be pushed away as a negative and regressive pull, and when should it have its way so it can lead into a
new place? The question can always be asked as to whether the
distraction seems to be serving $+100$ egocentric patterns or
whether it seems to be speaking for a "dark brother," some unknown and/or lost part such as the clown image was for the
man described above.

Only slowly does a person learn to communicate with these
inner parts, only slowly does he learn to listen. Resistances
raised because of shadow figures can be almost as unconquer-
able as the shadow itself, and often only the most patient, per-
severant, and creative use of meditative techniques and/or
analysis can deal with them.

In the previously mentioned Navaho Indian story of He-Who-
Teaches-Himself, at one point in his river journey the hero is
stopped by being pulled below the surface of the river into the
house of Water Monster. When he is finally rescued by the gods
of the earth and sky, he and these deities start to return to his
raft when the plopping sound of Frog, coming behind them,
halts them. Frog says: "Why do you go so quickly? Don't you
know you must first take away the spell we laid on you? Otherwise you will always have the water sickness. You must learn
how to make our prayer sticks and how to paint them in the
right colors. You must teach the man always to make a sacrifice
to us in his ceremonies." [75]

Frog is symbolically the spokesman for the most creative
values of the dark powers below the waters. His words point up
many things to be remembered about the depths, and about resistances, distractions, regressions, and shadow manifestations.
He is, in effect, saying: Why do you try to run away from what
is in the depths? Unless you attend to these things, they will

make you sick. But these dark powers have their particular healing qualities, if you learn of them, and sacrifice your narrow ego defenses. You are the child of the below as well as of the above. Remember that.

15

THE STUFF HE'S MADE OF

To hear the body's truths

"The body—and sex—are our first and our last living realities. Our soul is contained in them. We must love and respect them." [76] These words say clearly that the final psychological goal of Self can be achieved only within the substance of our finitude. It is not possible that man can work at his psychological-religious journey of orienting toward wholeness, without including these first and last living realities. And, despite modern attitudes, thousands of contemporary educated Western Europeans, and especially Americans, are still apologetic and uncomfortable about their bodies. (Some indicators of this awkwardness are the euphemisms for toilet, i.e., powder room, rest room, lounge!) There is a tendency to be embarrassed by sexuality and bodily needs, whereas youthful vigor, athletic prowess, and erotica are glorified.

On the other hand, within this last third of the twentieth century an enormous shift is taking place with regard to attitudes toward the body and sex as intrinsic and worthwhile parts of human as well as of subhuman existence. The pendulum is swinging and will continue to swing farther and farther from the turn-of-the-century denial of the body—or at least from the cleavage between body and mind and spirit. With the erosion of the meaningfulness of one-sided Christian virtues and values, and with the increase of knowledge about psychosomatic relationships, man has begun to include his body in what he is and in what he does. In Western society especially, with its relative affluence and physical satisfactions far beyond much of the rest of the world, the body is becoming almost a cult object. Mass communications and advertising media continually emphasize bodily enhancement and comfort. More and more stress is being placed on the body qua body in many psychological groups via such methods as the use of body contact and/or nudity as in themselves the way to self-knowledge. Sexual "freedom" as an end in itself is exploited in a variety of ways, particularly since the advent of birth control pills and intrauterine devices.

The truths of the body should be included in the progress toward wholeness, and from this standpoint the contemporary attitudes are healthy as antidotes to the point of view so long held. The body does not, however, contain the *entire* truth of an individual! Therefore many of the current methods seem to the authors rather less mature than they could be, and thus considerably less related to the wholeness of the Self than their users think they are. If the denial of and repression of bodily responses is destructive, as it certainly has been and is, so also is the concentration on bodily responses as if they were the ultimate goal of human self-reflective being. Man's sexuality belongs not only to his body, but to his mind and spirit. It can be one of the deep ways of communication, spiritual as well as physical, when man uses it as an expression of genuine love—love that has been worked at consciously as belonging to the larger Purpose. It is this sort of self-reflective consciousness about sexual expression which one sees in truly creative marriages. When sex is unrelated to the psychic and spiritual dimensions it becomes an egocentric gratification only, where each person

treats the other as an It and not as a Thou. When it becomes a
major driving force it is a neurotic compulsion like any other.
Such a compulsion can be transformed into creative feeling only
if it is drawn into the Ground of Being and seen to be one possible expression of the love of an I for a Thou. It is just possible that a sense of having lost our direction as persons, and
lost it to the dictatorship of technology, drives us to the asser-
tion of our bodies as the only thing we possess. This need not
be destructive if we can let strength of body truth assist us toward a repossession of heart, soul, mind. Destructiveness comes
if we try to force the body alone to carry the Self.

To master the stuff he is made of—not to beat it into a repressed subjection, not to make it into a singular god to be wor-
shiped—is what man needs to do as he lives his wholeness in
body as well as in spirit. There are a few excellent teachers of
body awareness and man's relationship to it.[77] There are far
too many untrained people capitalizing on this body cult up-
surge, offering "courses" in Yoga, in breathing techniques, in
esoteric ways of bodily relaxation through contact, etc. All we
propose to do is to set forth a few of the methods that we believe can be used without danger by individuals as supplementary to their total work of self-exploration.

The truth is that unless a person has at least a minimal working relationship between substance and spirit, body and psyche,
the chances for full and healing self-realization are not good.
Man must learn the joy of living in his body. An experienced
psychotherapist can often recognize the state of the psyche of
the client by recognizing the state of the body, for archetypes
manifest in soma as in psyche. Is the body flabby or tight?
Drooping or rigid? Filled with sighs? Twitches? How does
breath come? Voice? Any or all of these, and many others,
show on the outside what is going on inside. The psyche/soma
relationship is complex, so that to be sure which is chicken and
which is egg is almost impossible. This is related to Jung's work
on the "psychoid factor." [78] We can be fairly sure, however, that
hurry and shallow breathing and taut muscles are hindrances in
working at any of the techniques described herein. "The earth

produces of itself, first the blade, then the ear, then the full grain in the ear." (Mark 4:28.) These words of Jesus describe the way in which the unconscious realizations can grow if there is a good interrelationship between psyche and soma. Events cannot be forced to happen inside. A person can, however, permit a climate to exist wherein they may occur.

What, then, can the individual safely do alone? First of all, he can let his dedicated ego take the initiative in an act of *centering down,* of cultivating an attitude of bodily repose. This may consist of sitting quietly and listening to music that helps him to grow still. It may be a soundless sitting. Usually he needs to be aware of where the body is tense and of where the mind is racing, and in being aware he may be able to let go by allowing breathing to become easier as it finds its own rhythm. The teachers referred to earlier agree that for Western man one of the major areas of body tension is the place where the head and the rest of the body meet—neck and shoulders. It is as if for most people the conscious (head) and the unconscious (torso) clash instead of cooperate. Thus this centering process, simple though it may be, is of inestimable value in removing blocks to the flow of psychic energy.

Another step that can be taken is to *find out what our body image is.* How do I visualize myself? As ugly, awkward, too tall, too short, too fat, too thin, very graceful, seductive, virile, strong, weak, etc.? More often than not the body image is not faithful to what we really are in our bodily form, and if we are willing to be open to a new evaluation of the body we then become willing to open to a new evaluation of our psyche. The person's unconscious, after all, exists within the body. And an awareness of the total body and how it is experienced, as well as how it is, can be of great assistance in coming to terms with totality.

Such methods as working in clay or in finger paints have their physical concomitants, and it is important to be aware of the bodily aspects of such creating, as well as of the psychological aspects.

In work both with individuals and with groups we have found

one of the most easily usable methods of relating to the body is *moving to music*. *Not* dancing, *not* gymnastics, but moving to music. The music chosen can be of an infinite variety, but it is well to choose the kind that will best cut through whatever the day has held of tension, or depression, or hurry, or dullness. Primitive drums or other music having a definite and full beat often can set the body free from its mechanical tightness. Joyful music can cut through physical lethargy. Romantic composers can lead away from the sterile intellect, whereas classical composers can often help to still the ravages of negative emotions. This is an area where each person must experiment freely with all sorts of music and all sorts of body movements until he learns what will most help him to bring his psyche and his body into a friendly relationship. Moving to music is a method that can be used alone or in the company of others. When with others—whether with members of the family or with friends—it is important that there be no watchers. Participation of all those present is essential, for inhibitions about bodily movements are so great that one inevitably either tightens up or begins to "perform," if there are spectators. When the method is used by an individual, there are no ground rules. Pick your music. Move. In a dark room by candlelight. In sunlight. And in whatever way your own body and psyche tell you. This has nowhere been more delightfully described than by William Carlos Williams, in his poem "Danse Russe":

> If I when my wife is sleeping
> and the baby and Kathleen
> are sleeping
> and the sun is a flame-white disc
> in silken mists
> above shining trees,—
> if I in my north room
> dance naked, grotesquely
> before my mirror
> waving my shirt round my head
> and singing softly to myself:

"I am lonely, lonely.
I was born to be lonely,
I am best so!"
If I admire my arms, my face
my shoulders, flanks, buttocks
against the yellow drawn shades,—

Who shall say I am not
the happy genius of my household? [79]

The use of what we have called pantomime leads to a wider self-insight that includes the body's truths. In this method the starting stimulus can be a poem or part of a poem, a dream scene, a scene from a myth or from a parable, a painting, a sculpture—anything from art or from dream that has had affect. In addition to reflecting upon it, it is literally acted out in pantomime. If you are alone, you can try this at any time. We have found, however, that if this is to be done with a group, it is better done in semidarkness so that each can have his individual experience and then, after a specified and indicated interval, return to the group. It is startling to see how intensely involved people get in the feeling as well as in the meaning of whatever stimulus (art work, dream, mythic scene, parable) has been presented. Including the body's movements obviously adds great scope to the inner experience, as many verbal reports have indicated.

To hear the body's truths sounding in the psyche, to use "the stuff he's made of" in order better to serve his growing—this is for man to let the spirit and the substance join together in love and in Love.

16

THE PRIMARY WORD
I-THOU CAN BE SPOKEN...

Dialogue as inner and outer encounter

Dialogue has proved itself to be one of the most comprehensive and flexible ways to work on the widening of personality. We have developed dialogue, during many years of experimenting in seminars, as a method usable by any individual (whether or not in analysis), in the form of inner encounter with known or unknown inner or outer figures.

The word "dialogue" we use much as it is used by Buber in his I-Thou descriptions, but have expanded its use to encompass an added dimension. For Buber, the eternal Thou overarches and underlies every individual Thou. Also, Buber believes that one man can approach another as a Thou even though the other approaches him as an It. Therefore *dialogue* is always a possibility in any outer situation if one's own attitude is creative. The authors extend the use of the "primary word I-Thou" to include inner persons—images within the psyche—as well as outer persons, because it is hard to understand how the psyche can be excluded from the total Meaning. If it is included, then those who walk across the *inner* stage are as needful of dialogue as those who walk across the *outer* stage.

Mary T. is trying to overcome her hatred of her mother. Part of the solution lies in her ability to dialogue with her mother, to speak the primary word I-Thou. At the same time Mary has nightmares of an evil man who tries to kill her. Unless she can learn to speak the word *I-Thou* to him as well as to her mother, she will possibly never totally resolve the mother problem. This is because the inner "he" encounters Mary not only in dreams but at those times when she is, in her own words, "lashed by a demon" against her mother and she must speak with this demon or destroy and be destroyed.

To speak this primary word *I-Thou,* whether to the eternal Thou, to a fellowman, or to part of oneself, is to enter into a "life of dialogue." A person takes a stand in relation to that to which he says Thou. Thus to dialogue is to love. To dialogue is "to be seized by the power of exclusiveness." There is an inner world of objective reality (what Jung calls the "objective psyche") and an outer world of objective reality. Both worlds want responses from man. He can more easily see how the outer calls to him. But he must not forget his dreams, or the legends and folktales that describe bewitched persons imprisoned in trees, stoves, dungeons, or animal shapes, persons that are crying out to be heard and loved. In a tale from Grimm, she who willingly serves the ugly and frightening Mother Holle is rewarded. Found throughout Europe is the folktale about a serpent—or frog—who has to be kissed in order to be transformed. These servings and lovings are, in essence, kinds of dialogue. There are in fact, as dreams and folktales make clear, many inner voices of the psyche to be listened to and to be followed into new places where the Thou resides.

Dialogue, then, is a method where both parties are involved in an I-Thou confrontation. From the human side, to enter dialogue requires a creative *I*. A creative *I* is one that can focus intensely on its relationship to the *Thou*—whether the ultimate Thou, the Thou as another person or as the value in the moment, or the specific Thou that emerges from the unconscious and wants to be integrated. In order for a real dialogue to take place, the *I* needs: work on egocentricity; listening; attentive observation to the reality of the *Thou* being encountered; and a desire to serve whatever new value emerges from the dialogue. In any monologue there is only one point of view. In dialogue there is the assumption that two points of view exist, that of the *I* and that of something else, and together in the primary word *I-Thou,* they witness to Purpose. If, as we said earlier, all growth comes about through bipolarities, and if all choice is based upon the fact of ambivalence, then every Thou—ultimate, immediate, or inner—has within it its own bipolarity and also, at its core, a need for redemption. The Lord God wants to be confronted, known, loved. The neighbor wants this. The Self within man wants this. It is because of these "wants" that the creative *I* must consciously enter into the primary word *I-Thou,* into dialogue. The discoveries that come from such dialogues not only enlarge one's reality and authenticity as a person, but increase one's ability to function in life relationships with love.

Do not confuse the *dialogue method* with what is usually called "inner dialogue"—an aimless, often intense and preoccupying conversation in our head with a person or a situation with which we are at odds. This sort of "conversation" is monologue, not dialogue, and usually acts as a distraction. Second, do not assume that the *dialogue method,* when carried out adequately, can be done only in the head. It must involve the word "concretized," whether written, spoken aloud, painted, sung, or danced. Without this, involvement is difficult, if not impossible.

If dialogue is to be utilized as one adequate method for insight and growth, these elements need to be included: an ego with a desire and a willingness to open the doors to whatever "stranger" may come, and the ability to say to him the primary word I-Thou; a humility that will enable one to hear the other, and a courage that can reply; the patience and perseverance to stay with what may start out as a debate until it grows into a discussion and becomes a creation; and, finally, the careful recording of these encounters in writing, or in painting or clay, so that they will not be forgotten.

The following dialogue, excerpted from the journal of a

woman who was trying to understand and free herself from negativity related to her father who had left his family when the woman was in her early adolescence, will illustrate:

ME: You ruined my mother's life! All our lives! Why did you have to do such a thing?
FATHER: Why shouldn't I have?
ME: That proves what Mother always said—that men are no good, that they take what they want and leave.
FATHER: Does that prove she was right?
ME: Of course! Didn't you do just that? You left her. You left all of us, me and my sister and my brother. And she had to bring us up all by herself.
FATHER: Well, she had lots of help. Her mother. The big house. More than enough money.
ME: But she suffered so much. She cried so much. And she got sick and had all those terrible headaches. That was your fault.
FATHER: Was it? Do you think she really loved me?
ME: Of course.
FATHER: How do you know? Did she show it? Was she warm to me when I came home at night? Or didn't she complain at me, pick at me, tell me what I ought to do, what Joe had done for his wife? Didn't she?
ME: Oh, I hate you! I hate you!
FATHER: Well, didn't she? Be honest. Didn't she?

At this point the woman stopped the dialogue. After a few days she realized, as she read it again, that an entirely new dimension of the relationship between her parents was making itself known and that, in all honesty, she did not want to face it. She then carried this dialogue forward in several different ways. She recorded further conversations between herself and her father. She had the exciting experience of a dialogue by way of clay modeling—making a crude head of her mother and one of her father (she was not an artist) and talking with them together. The father's head, she felt, was "nicer," "had more love on its face." The mother's head was "sharp and witchy" and she didn't like it.

Because parents are so often involved in the things that have gone wrong, dialogues with them in this way are among the most necessary and the most helpful. (And here dialogue becomes trio-logue.) The degree to which such dialogue is successful depends upon sincerity of purpose and the willingness of the person to stay with it. For instance, if a person has been taught always to love everyone, including his parents, and has therefore repressed all his other feelings and been suffocated under "ought" and "should" and "goodness," it is far from easy to have dialogues that express resentment and hostility toward those who have helped to undermine his identity. Not only can he not do it in the outer world with people he resents, but it takes all the courage he has to try it in the inner world.

In addition to parents, outer and inner, another subject for the dialogue method is one's egocentric image. A middle-aged woman who discovered a tyrant in herself, a dominating image that ruled the household, husband and children and all, named this inner tyrant Bloody Mary. She made Bloody Mary in clay and smashed her to bits. She drew Bloody Mary and tore her up. But all these dialogues were done with a feeling for Bloody Mary as a Thou rather than as an It, so that in the end Bloody Mary was subdued rather than repressed, and her energy was turned into creative channels. In much the same way many creation myths tell how, when a monster is killed, its body is turned into rivers, trees, animals, winds, and grain.

If there is an inner censor (one person named this part of himself the Tormentor) who is forever making one feel guilty, incompetent, worthless, it is illuminating to engage this part in a dialogue, too. And it may be a dialogue in which a person has to stand up to a figure that has long held power over him. Emma Jung said to one of the authors, "We must get to the place where we can tell that part of us which makes us feel guilty to go and peddle his potatoes somewhere else!" Or there may be a Big Baby in us who continually tries to pull away from discipline and ultimate concern, leading into self-indulgences and compulsions of various kinds. It too can be talked with and brought into adulthood. The destructive shadow sides need to have the primary word I-Thou spoken to them, in order to bring them into creative relationship.

Myth, parable, story, legend—these are rich sources for the discovering of figures and situations that move in man. To the degree that they move him they provide him with dialogical partners, because myths, parables, stories, and legends draw upon unconscious levels of personality and mirror what goes on interiorly. This is one reason for the use of parable in teaching, and for the ritual reenactment of myths. Much can be learned about hidden parts of personality by a dialogue with some mythical, legendary, or fictional character who arouses either positive or negative feelings. For example, in such a tale as Mother Holle, referred to earlier, a person can find the wicked stepmother inside and carry on a dialogue with her, or can do the same with the helpful stepdaughter, or her lazy and egocentric half sister. What would the selfish one say? How can I talk with my inner negative stepmother? Could I have a trio-logue? Another example, out of the many that could be given, is the previously discussed parable of the good Samaritan. The various characters in the parable can be interiorized and brought into dialogue. What kind of a conversation will ensue between my inner Priest-Levite and myself? Between my Wounded Man and me? What can I say to my inner Samaritan and he to me? If all talk together, what will the outcome be? What will happen if I make my Wounded Man in clay, or paint him, and then let him speak to me?

We have also used dialogue to explore the nature of prejudice and to find ways to change it. That race, or religion, or social attitude most difficult to face can be personified by some member of it, i.e., a Japanese, a Roman Catholic, a John Bircher, an Indian, a Baptist, a Communist, and so on. Often such figures appear in dreams. In the same way as in any other dialogue, this person must be brought into open inner discussion, must be listened to as well as talked to. Can he or she be thought of as a Thou rather than as an It? Above all, he must be recognized as a Thou that exists *inside* as well as (or instead of) outside. That this is so is demonstrated in every dream about persons of other racial, religious, or social groups, because one's dreams are about oneself. The social implications of this use of dialogue are many. There is, so to say, inner prejudice as well as outer, an inner United Nations as well as an outer one, and both require openness, patience, listening, trying to communicate, if the disparate members are to meet. The inner UN can help the outer UN. If, for instance, I find in myself, by way of dream or folktale, poetry or fiction, a character of the type I am most prejudiced against, and *if I work to have dialogue with that disliked inner part of me,* the chances are that my outer attitudes will enable me better to deal with an outer evil —as in the case of fascism—because I have dealt with an inner one. Or, on the other hand, because I have accepted an inner part of me that previously I have despised, I may be well on the way to a new outer relationship.

No matter who or what is the "other" in dialogue, no matter whether the "other" is a loved or a hated being, only as a Thou must it be brought into the presence of an I. "All real living is meeting," says Buber. Meeting includes speaking the primary word *I-Thou* to the manifold persons of the interior world just as surely as to those of the exterior world. If man speaks only the primary word *I-It* to the inner being or to the outer being, he cannot expect to have relationship or wholeness. There is an infinite variety of persons with whom he can dialogue, and it is for each person to discover which ones come first for him at any given time in his growth.

17

THE LOG
IN YOUR OWN EYE

*Projection can be
a tool for self-discovery*

Man is both jealous of his freedom and frightened to death of his uniqueness. As a consequence of bouncing between fear and jealousy, he hardly knows where he ends and others begin. Out of his fear or his jealousy he blames all threats to his freedom on others, or he accuses others of forcing him to be free. Desiring his own depths and wanting to run from them simultaneously, he spends enormous time and energy either loving or hating his psychic realities outside himself. In short, man projects, seeing on an outer screen of persons or events what properly belongs in him.

"Why do you see the speck that is in your brother's eye," asked Jesus, "but do not notice the log that is in your own eye?" (Matt. 7:3.) The problem of log and speck has been around for a very long time. It still beclouds relationships of all kinds. It is still hard to see because, for the most part, it so convincingly belongs "out there." Gerald Heard, writing more than forty years ago, anticipated the contemporary scene and its struggles and projections:

> We shall see the violences of this profound conflict, by those who suffer from them, thrown out into the outer world of action. We shall see the outer violences of class wars, experts' wars, nations' wars and the age-group wars—all projections of inner conflict striving to avoid the crisis that must be fought out in itself. But in the end the force within us, which we are now attempting to get rid of by our violent actions in the world without, will turn in upon ourselves. For we are not answering its demand that we should change ourselves by these our violent efforts to overset the world.[80]

Heard anticipated the warnings of Jung. That is, *we see outside ourselves,* in other persons, nations, in objects and images, *qualities and/or powers that are actually* (only, or also) *in our own psyches,* belonging to us.

In literature, one of the splendid descriptions of the tragic consequences of unconscious projection is in Shakespeare's play *Othello.* The protagonist, Othello, sees in his beloved Desdemona all his own gentle and feminine qualities, while she sees in him her warlike masculine side. Of him she says:

> If I be left behind,
> A moth of peace, and he go to the war,
> The rites for which I love him are bereft me.

He says of her:

> where I have garner'd up my heart,
> Where either I must live, or bear no life;
> The fountain from the which my current runs,
> Or else dries up.[81]

These high phrases are representative of so many "in-love-nesses" that one is tempted to smile indulgently. But if such unconscious projections are left unconscious, to gather to themselves more and more powerful archetypal energy, they frequently lead to disaster, as they did for Othello. Because Othello failed to see or to deal with his projections, he destroyed all that he loved. If what a man does not know of himself is always projected—as in the case of Othello—then only the understanding and redirecting of his projections can help him to survive and grow. This involves knowing *that* he projects, *what* he projects, and *how* to use his projections for expanding his own consciousness.

How can a person know that he projects? It is very difficult to recognize and to accept. If he downgrades himself, it is unthinkable that those excellences which he sees in others are anywhere else but in those others! If he overvalues himself, the inferior qualities that he finds in his neighbors obviously belong to them. (He may function sometimes one way, sometimes the other.) But given a true commitment to growth, combined with honesty, he can break through his illusion and recognize that he is projecting. He can begin by asking and answering these questions: Do I have excessively emotional reactions to people, reactions that are disproportionate to the situation and that occur over and over in the same kind of situation or with the same kind of person? Do I ever have sudden uprushes that catch me unaware—whether the emotion be anger, fear, tears of joy or sorrow? Have I ever felt that I "couldn't live without" some person? Or that I "couldn't endure" to be around someone? Do I feel that almost everyone who is (black, white, educated, uneducated, outgoing, withdrawn, married, unmarried, Republican, Democrat, etc.) must be (unpleasant, dangerous, stupid, not my equal, better than I, etc.)? In some situations or with certain people, do I have a gnawing sense that there are things which I cannot see, as if I were enclosed in a fog that clouds my perception? If the answer to any of these questions is Yes, then projection is probably operating. The truth is, of course, that everyone projects some of the time and in some situations.

Projections can be made onto parents, children, husbands, wives, siblings, ministers, teachers, bosses, religious leaders, political leaders, actors and actresses, friends, and many others. Men permit their feminine aspects to be carried for them by women, and women let their masculine aspects be carried by men. At the assassinations of men such as President Kennedy, Martin Luther King, Robert Kennedy, Malcolm X, Mahatma Gandhi, the enormity of what thousands of people have let such men carry is manifested clearly in emotional responses. Being "in love" is a condition of projection, where the other person carries, temporarily at least, almost all psychological and religious meanings. People who live only for their children are in reality projecting onto the children the meaning of their own lives. In analysis, the patient projects onto the analyst many of the things that must eventually be faced, from the most negative to the most positive.

There are several ways to begin to delineate *what* is being projected. Written exploration of projection is much better than just thinking about it. A good practice is to write out the following: people with whom I am most uncomfortable; people with whom I am happiest; people that I fear (or resent or distrust); public figures that I most admire; ones that I most dislike; people I would most want to be like; people that I would not want to be like; any other categories of persons not represented here. For each of the persons or groups of persons listed, try to analyze what traits or qualities you believe they have that makes you feel as you do about them, and write this in a parallel column. Then, in a third column, write out ways in which you may possess in yourself what these people seem to possess.

For example, a young minister who believed himself to be filled with Christian love and charity, and who hated people who were not, listed Rasputin, the "mad monk" of Russia, as someone he very much looked down upon. And in filling in the despicable qualities of Rasputin, the minister found that these were in fact qualities that his friends—and even some of his more courageous parishioners—had been hinting at as belonging to him. Or, at an opposite end of the spectrum, there was the self-effacing woman who held the lowest opinion of her own gifts and put down people such as Albert Schweitzer, Abraham

Lincoln, Madam Pandit as having what she would like to have. She was deeply moved and surprised when it was pointed out to her that she did have the same kind of loving creativity in many of her relationships.

Culver Barker once said, "We do unto others what we have not done for ourselves." [82] This is very pertinent to the subject of projection—especially with regard to parents and teachers, but also with regard to ministers, doctors, psychotherapists. What we have failed to express, or have overexpressed, what we have not solved, have left hidden—these are the things we "do unto others." It is crucial that parents write out what they feel and think about children—their expectations, annoyances, evaluations, hopes. Be aware of how your children appear in your dreams. Are the children being forced to be what the parents were not? Are parents disliking in children what in reality should be worked at in themselves? These are some of the most destructive ways in which projection operates from parent to child—or from teacher to pupil. Sometimes it goes from one marriage partner to the other, or from friend to friend. A divorced woman dreamed that her older son, then about seven, appeared at the door of her room wearing her husband's clothes. He was all but engulfed in a suit far too big for him, with only his eyes and forehead visible above the coat collar. She was able to see that she had been projecting onto him all the manhood qualities her husband had taken from her, and was able then to begin to take this inside herself and away from the boy.

How can one *deal with* projections once he knows *that* he projects, and knows also something of *what* he projects? If the bulges and hollows are to be seen and changed, the individual needs to find interiorly what he has previously seen only exteriorly. This means asking the right questions. In this kind of dialogue—where one begins to talk with those inner voices which have heretofore only been heard in other people—there are questions to be asked and helpful answers to be heard.

Mrs. M. H. found that she disliked a surprisingly large number of people whom she labeled "aggressive," and felt that she was "picked on" and "pushed around." Then she began to ask such questions as: "Why do I react against aggressive people so strongly? Is it because I am that way myself and won't admit it? In that case I'd better find out and do something about it! Or is it that I'm too weak, and resent others doing what I can't do? And if that is so, I guess I need to learn to assert myself." Mrs. M. H. began to see that others seemed less aggressive as she herself developed her own self-confidence and could state her needs and wishes.

Another example is Max L. Emotional people—including his young wife—got increasingly on his nerves, so that not only his marriage but several other personal relationships were threatened. He knew his father had branded any expression of feeling as being "womanish," but he didn't see where he was involved until a friend pointed out to him that he always got tears in his eyes whenever the theme of "woman with child" came up, and also that his voice often broke when he spoke of such things as love, or music, or death. By following these insights, Max discovered his warm and tender side and was able to let it live.

Two further considerations about projection: in addition to taking it inside, to what extent should an individual involve the persons on whom he has projected? And, on the other hand, what can he—or should he—do when he feels someone is projecting onto him something that isn't true of him? Whether or not to involve the other depends on many factors, and no general rule is possible. When we share our struggle with the other person we risk our self-images and expose ourselves to being known, which may be a helpful thing to do. But we can as easily be tempted to discharge our feelings too quickly by dumping them in an uncreative "confessional." Too many groups today are based on this dumping of unconscious projections by people talking *at* each other, by putting un-understood and unresolved affects onto one another and thus never individually working them out. Sometimes the healthiest possible step is to work it through with the other, with sensitivity and ethical judgment. Sometimes nothing would be gained in this way. Sometimes outright harm could be done. Sometimes the most necessary and most creative thing to do is to hold what has been learned by seeing the projection, containing it within the vessel of the psyche as within a womb, and letting it come slowly to birth in a transformed and nonprojected way.

Finally, what can be done if the log seems truly to be in the other's eye? How you seem may be another's problem. If you are a parent, for example, you can be perceived by your children as hero or heroine carrying life's highest values forward, or as a misguided but harmless old fool who doesn't know about things, or as a dictator who inhibits fun and throttles joy. Teachers, ministers, psychotherapists, bosses, may receive projections of wisdom, healing, leadership, or of overdiscipline, bungling, self-righteousness, and domination. Friends or spouses can be made into carriers of any opposite that remains unconscious in the relationship.

When such things happen to any of us—parents, teachers, ministers, therapists—there are several steps we can take. The crucial first step is to ask whether or not we do in fact have some of the quality being projected onto us. If we do, then we need to see if we are misusing it in some way. We may, in our role, have to set boundaries, but are we doing it in anger, or objectively? We may be forgetful sometimes, but are we using this to avoid situations, and therefore being perceived as rejecting? And even if we are creative and spontaneous, we must take care that we permit others to be spontaneous as well. In any event, whether the projection we receive is positive or negative, and even if we find we have given no cause for it, we need to maintain objectivity. A person is rarely as fine or as dreadful as others see him. It goes without saying that if we do find we have given some cause for projection, we need to be conscious about it and work at it inside.

Whether we are working at the projections we place onto others, or on those they place onto us, we should above all try to do so within the framework of intentionality, of concern for wholeness. If such work is done with patience, humbleness, honesty, courage, and the desire to bring all that can be brought from unconsciousness into conscious availability, the depths of the projected collective unconscious can be used for the fuller manifestation of Life and for Wholeness.

18

IN PARTNERSHIP

Analysis and the role of dreams

The methods we have described and discussed generally have been ones that can be used by almost any person regardless of his circumstances. However, it is essential to point out that there are limits to what one can do by oneself, and that there are depths in a person that he cannot safely encounter without the assistance of a trained analyst. As Kunkel wrote:

> Seek a helper. It may seem paradoxical to think of self-education as involving the need of outside help. Yet the fact is . . . that a helper is sometimes necessary and the most practical thing to do is to seek one. After all, it must be obvious, that even with the aid of the helper much depends upon one's own efforts at self-education.[83]

We believe that it is possible for self-knowledge to go a great distance alone if it goes with integrity of an ego dedicated to a larger-than-egocentric Meaning. Nonetheless, there are blinders to spiritual vision and resistances to growth, and when these are great enough, someone will be needed to help. Here psy-

chotherapy is a major instrument. Psychotherapy (analysis) is
a necessary tool on several counts. Sometimes the thickness of
man's defensive resistance is so great that he cannot break
through unaided. Or there is the overwhelming sense of guilt
that demands confession and a confessor. There is the fact that
often another can see in a man what he cannot see himself.
Time after time the analyst has to be "the lawyer for the unconscious"—meaning that the analyst must plead (even if word-
lessly) for the richness of the deeper layers of the unconscious,
for the value of getting to them, and for the specific under-
privileged, lost parts of the psyche needing to be given a chance
for life. But beyond these, it is the numinous and deeply compelling power of the Self, as the immanent God-image, that
forces a person to analysis.

These mysterious, deep levels of the collective unconscious,
where the archetypes are in continual ebb and flow, usually
cannot be explored either fully or safely without a guide. The
analyst lends loving support and a practiced hand as the individual moves into the "non-ego" or objective psyche to encounter both those psychic elements which have been repressed
and also those archetypal powers which can lead either to
transformation or to disintegration. The great artists have moved
into this realm—not always safely—and have returned it to
mankind in all its terror and loveliness. Madmen have been lost
there. Both have shown that opposites must be dealt with if
man is to be whole. Some of these can be fully encompassed and
brought into relationship only in analysis. The analytic process,
when entered into wholeheartedly by analyst and patient alike, is
one of the richest and most exciting adventures of relationship
and exploration that can be experienced. Analytic sessions are
the containing vessels within which the Cry can be heard, and
from which the wondrous new life can be born. Analysis is
uniquely helpful when the process known as "transference" is
set in motion. A person puts onto (transfers to) the analyst
complexes and archetypal contents that otherwise could not
be known. Transference thus is

a phenomenon by which the patient becomes aware of psychic functions in general that have been lacking in his conscious life. Generally speaking, transference is not only a mechanism for the re-experience of repressed infantile sexual impulses, but a tool with the help of which the patient can integrate so far unrealized psychic faculties. In this way the transference can help the patient become aware of unconscious contents, which are needed for future development, that is, for the process of individuation.[84]

Transference is often cultivated by the analyst—and is usually used by the analyst when it happens—for the revealing and channeling of the fertile unconscious depths. It is to be distinguished from projection, which is the putting outside of oneself whatever is unknown—positive or negative. In transference, the process is utilized consciously by the analyst for healing. It is apparent that transference becomes a religious technique insofar as it is future-oriented in its concern for the unrealized potentialities of the individual. It is as if the values of the deeper Self were carried consciously by the analyst for the individual until he can see them, accept them as his, and carry them for himself.

In addition to helping a person with his blind spots and being the container of his unconscious values, analysis works with dreams in a way that the person is unable to work with them alone. Because dreams and their symbols are so vital to self-understanding, and because their meanings are often veiled by human one-sidedness, it is easy to see why analysis facilitates dealing with them. One can—and should—keep a record of dreams whether or not he is in analysis. There are ways that a person can relate to dreams by himself, but working with dreams in analysis adds dimensions of understanding that are impossible to achieve alone.

The religious function of the ego is, among other things, to work with the material of the non-ego in the direction of the Self. Within the framework of analysis it is much more possible to do this with dream material because analysis provides the objectivity of the analyst to assist in the discrimination between egocentric interpretations of dream symbols and interpretations that are closer to the truth the unconscious is trying to tell. This truth is exceedingly powerful, and can either destroy or build, depending upon how it is used. An erroneous interpretation of a message from the depths (via dreams) can lead not only far afield but even into personal disaster. Therefore we believe there is great danger in persons trying to interpret their dreams alone—or in groups—because of the blindnesses and projections and lacks of objectivity that do more harm than good.

It is important to stress that every one of the many methods described and discussed in the various chapters of Part 2 can be creative adjuncts to analysis, as well as ways of self-exploration for persons working alone. The climate of psychological search is changing, and many subjects are today commonly shared in nonprofessional situations that heretofore would only have been spoken behind the closed doors of an analyst's consulting room. Analysts and laymen alike are being stretched beyond old boundaries. Further discussion of the process of analysis, and its value, is not relevant here. That the authors believe it to be valuable, and in most cases essential, for the deepest self-exploration (not to mention the absolute need for it in extreme neurosis and in psychosis) is evidenced by the fact that both authors are themselves analysts.

19

THE INMOST LAND

*Various ways
of meditation
and introversion*

If man wants to come to himself, whole, if he is going to where he needs to go to be authentically who he is, he has to know his interior world. If self-reflective consciousness is man's highest evolutionary reach, it must encompass the "inmost land," described by May Sarton:

> Sometimes it seems to be the inmost land
> All children still inhabit when alone.
> They play the game of morning without end,
> And only lunch can bring them, startled, home
> Bearing in triumph a small speckled stone.
> . . . .
> It is, perhaps, our most complex creation,
> A lovely skill we spend a lifetime learning,
> Something between the world of pure sensation
> And the world of pure thought, a new relation,
> As if we held in balance the globe turning.[85]

To work with the inmost land is to hold "in balance the globe" of larger Meaning with the archetypal deeps included. We have already discussed some techniques for relating to this inner world. There are some other techniques that have proved their usability and effectiveness: vertical meditation, meditative introversion, confessional meditation, active imagination, artwork.

The first step is the evoking or arousing or calling forth of whatever symbol is to be worked with. The symbol reveals the contents of the unconscious in dreams, through those objects, persons, and situations that draw emotions and energies to them, in mythic, parabolic, poetic, and religious statements, and through art forms of all kinds. Regardless of which of the methods is used, work with all of them has shown that the arousal of the unconscious merely as unconscious is not only not always sufficient but is, in many cases, dangerously insufficient. It is not that a direction must be forced or made, but that unless an ego is involved in a choice to work with the unconscious for the sake of healing, the ego can easily be swallowed up by unconscious eruptions.

From ancient times up to and including contemporary religious practices, symbols and the rituals attending them have helped man to relate more deeply both to the Self and to the Presence behind and beyond the Self. The methods we are describing are ways of transition and change, of psychic and spiritual movement toward completion, and thus are related to certain phases of rites of initiation. Part of the mystery rites of ancient Greece were, for example: waiting for the right dream before being permitted entrance to the temple; being swaddled as an infant and then being lowered into a well to ponder on rebirth; being stripped naked before facing the gods or their representatives. C. A. Meier has written fully on Greek healing rites and their meaning to modern man.[86]

Ways of Meditation

We are not attempting to describe all the ways of classic meditation, Eastern or Western, with their steps of emptying, filling, purgation, illumination, and so on. This has been done excellently by Evelyn Underhill,[87] William Johnston,[88] Dorothy Phillips,[89] and others. We are not talking about a state of just letting things happen. Rather, we will describe here three ways of meditation which we have explored over the years and found helpful: *vertical meditation, meditative introversion, loose-rope and confessional meditation.*

Vertical meditation is the evocation of some major symbol by the ego, letting that symbol come to rest in an inner Center, where the ego then descends to be gripped by it. This silent verticality is on an ego-Self orientation. This provides an "altar" to which nodal points of psychic restlessness can be brought, held in quietness, illumined. There is where the "living flame of love" burns below the distractions, below the fears, below the doubts, and where the ego and the God-image may come close to each other even if only for a brief period. It is a focused and deep stillness, consciously experienced and integrated. It is an act wherein the ego turns toward some aspect of the in-dwelling God in order that an integration may be made possible. As a method it is indeed rewarding, even if not easy.

Meditative introversion is different from and yet related to vertical meditation. It is more nearly a practice of the presence of the unconscious in the way that Brother Lawrence meant the "practice of the presence of God." [90] Because it is a "practice" rather than a "happening," it is an act wherein the ego turns toward the inner world and its symbols in order that the Self can become more fully known and functional. It is the ego working as midwife to deliver from man's unknown depths the child of his becoming, authentic and responsive. It is a method to bring together consciousness and the unconscious, the inner movement and the outer situation, all under the aegis of the transcendent Meaning. How can it be used? Let us assume several things: that a person wants to work in the "inmost land" for the reasons of growth; that he is aware of some unidentifiable fear, obsessive thoughts about a person or situation, newly recognized angers toward parents, a joy that he cannot accept; that he already knows something about his egocentricity and how it can seduce him from further explorations. With these already present facts, the next step is to bring the problem prayerfully into the "laboratory."

Sarah M. knows that she is too precise and orderly, and that her feelings are not as available to her as she would like, or as her man friend would like. She has set aside an entire Sunday morning for herself, alone in her apartment. She has let go of the notions that she ought to be cleaning, or washing clothes, or writing letters. She has unplugged the telephone. Sarah's first step is to listen to a record that helps her to center down. As she sits quietly in the silence that follows the music, hoping that some door will open into the inner world and show her something as lovely as the music, she is startled and shocked to have an evil face of a man suddenly come into her interior seeing. Here is what she wrote in her journal later the same day:

> It was awful to see him. I almost shut him off. Until I recognized him—that nasty little man that I see on the way to work. Why do I dislike him so? Decided to bring him in—the mean face—and talk to him. My God, it was hard! I'm a real coward, I guess. The worst of it was when I realized that he was part of me! All the mean hateful part of me that beats my own child-like side when it's irrational and disorderly. He's the guy that makes things hard for Joe, I guess!

Sarah worked at this relationship with the symbolic inner figure in subsequent periods of meditative introversion. At one point she wrote:

> Poor Joe! He really gets it when my Mean Man moves in. It would serve me right if Joe told me off for good.

She came slowly to the realization that her Mean Man was her creative feeling as it had been cut off in childhood. Seeing this, she could begin to love "him" and "it." This love expanded her overall capacity to love and serve the larger Meaning, as well as her capacity to love the Self and her neighbor—including Joe.

Martin D.'s meditative introversion had to go in quite another direction. Martin's world was relatively chaotic. An illegitimate child of a mother who had wandered from city to city during his childhood, he had received little sense of his identity. His ego had a hard time of it. For him to become centered enough to risk letting his "inmost land" be seen required careful preparation by way of the word. Usually he began by reading aloud some phrase or sentence from a book. And when he was able to allow the images to rise up in him he learned to stop frequently and paint them and write words around and across the paintings to "explain" them. Thus his ego (the I) was in these ways strengthened, and in time he was able to permit the inner world a real relationship to his total life. Many other examples could be given. However, every case is unique and each person must discover his own opposites.

Loose-rope meditation is another way to follow a particular symbol. The symbol is "fastened" to the peg of intentions. Once it is securely fastened to its peg by the resolve to speak the primary word I-Thou, one can risk letting it go as one would let an animal go that was fastened to a stake by a long tether. The symbol can then wander off, in a combination of free association and amplification, for quite a distance. From time to time, however, it should be pulled back to its starting point— the intention—and then set free again. In this way the person does not, on the one hand, completely lose the symbol in a meandering maze, but on the other hand, he is letting it lead him more freely than he would in meditative introversion. For example, I may be haunted by a tune. I sit down with it, re-solved to learn what it wants of me. I try to remember what it is, and I try to hum it through and can't, which angers me, and I recall how my aunt used to hum off-key while she washed dishes.

I go into an imaginary scene of telling my aunt how this bothers me—which I never could actually have done. So I begin to build strength where heretofore I had been weak. At this point I realize where I have gone, recall my original intention and return to the tune. Four or five such wanderings may be necessary before I realize the deepest symbolic meaning of the tune which conjures up a rush of images totally opposed to where I had thought I was. By this loose-rope meditation I have come to a new insight about something I needed to see. I have also gained much more insight with each wandering and return.

With this method especially—although with the others as well—there is the continual danger that the inner censor will keep us from seeing what we need to see. This censor can be dealt with by always remembering it may be there, and by making the yes-saying to the Cry and to wholeness stronger than the censor's no-saying. A woman had this dream:

> In a large warehouse a man in a Nazi uniform jumps up, issuing orders and bobbing around like a crazy machine. He screams we all are to be killed, sticks a cannon in my face and fires. The cannon only gurgles and sags but I am terrified. Then I tell him all sorts of reasons why we shouldn't be killed.

It took a firm hand and much patience for the dreamer to permit this inner Nazi to wander, because her censor kept trying to force him into a place where he could be repressed.

Confessional meditation is the term that Fritz Kunkel used to describe a method of self-exploration under the aspect of the larger Meaning wherein man "confesses"—brings into the light —those tendencies and actions which weigh him down with guilt:

> If you repress what you harbor, you will be stifled by your own unlived life. If you express the repressed tendencies, you may destroy and kill. You must find another way. . . . The way out, indeed the only way out, as far as we know, is the way of confession. But the word confession must be understood, and

the method be used in the right way, according to the structure of the human mind and the special problems of our time.[91]

Kunkel goes on to point out that whereas a few decades ago confession was the prerogative of priest and minister, today neither they, nor even many psychological helpers, are equipped for "this dangerous work." If the confessor judges, repression ensues. If the confessor absolves, the darkness of the unconscious may never be really plumbed. Therefore very often the individual alone with himself must bring before the Presence of God those things which he most wants to run away from. He must remember that this Presence contains both conscious and unconscious elements, even as he does. Therefore, before this Presence man's *I* can see both its "secret sins" and its "buried talents." If a person works with this method in its full implications, he is immediately plunged into the problems of guilt, forgiveness, and healing. The new relationship must be between the *I* as conscious chooser and a *Thou who works also through the unconscious.* And this is "nothing short of a new revelation of God," as Hans Schaer says.[92] Confessional meditation is one way of implementing this.

Active Imagination

Active imagination is a term used specifically in Jungian analytical psychology to refer to an encounter between the ego and some symbol arising from the non-ego levels of the unconscious—or from what Jung calls the "objective psyche." In many ways active imagination closely resembles meditative introversion, with aspects similar to dialogue. Insofar as it is different, the difference resides in the degree of directedness as well as in the overall goal. It has been described by many analytical psychologists, including Barbara Hannah,[93] Gerhard Adler,[94] and Jung himself.[95] We refer the reader to these accounts. "The way is not without danger," as Jung says. We would underline this very emphatically. It is not an easy technique because it involves opening up the deepest layers of the unconscious, and because it involves these depths it also must involve the ability to handle these depths. One may work at this method via writing fantasies out, drawing or painting them, dancing them out, etc. One may begin with symbols from dream or follow a fantasy when it comes unbidden. Active imagination is both powerful and healing—especially healing when dealt with consciously and devotedly. And usually, we believe, it needs a helper.

Symbols and Art Media

There are two different ways in which art media and symbols can be combined to help toward the "inward land." The first is the better known. It is through responses to already created artistic forms—music, poetry, painting, sculpture, the dance, drama. The good artist (and whatever else we may mean by that word "good" we include authenticity as well as competence) has his trapdoors open to the fires that burn inside him, and the draft, which is caused from the open doors, comes out as his creation. If we respond to it, it becomes ours also because it helps us to open our trapdoors and release our draft. One can begin to explore spontaneous likes and dislikes as to kinds of music, painting, sculpture, drama, dance, and literature. (In this as in all else that is being used to further self-knowledge, it is well to write down what is learned as it occurs. Forgetting is one of the subtlest of resistances.) It must not be understood here that the goal is to like all things in the arts with equal fervor, even were it desirable. And it is not desirable. The goal of this method is the goal of expanding self-awareness so that parts of the psyche are not *excluded* for negative reasons and other parts *included* for negative reasons. The more a person becomes authentically himself, and more whole, the more he will be able to respond to a variety of creative expressions and to a variety of kinds of persons. The world will not be a neutral gray. The spectrum of colors has been increased.

Many kinds of questions can be asked about many kinds of media. What paintings do I most respond to in this exhibit? What ones upset me? Irritate me? In this play, who are the characters I identify or sympathize with? Who are the ones I dislike? Feel angry toward? What kinds of art expressions make me feel sad? Happy? Can I "hear" poetry, or does it bore me? Can I respond to primitive jazz music, or do I think it beneath me? What sort of novel do I most enjoy? Every sort of music has been recorded. Much introverted time can be spent with art books and photographs of sculpture and architecture. And questions can be asked in relationship to these, in solitude. One further value of responding to creations of artists is that, if they are authentic products of the artist's unconscious depth, they often bring a person closer to his own authenticity and wholeness because of their inherent unity of meaning.

The second method of using art media in relationship to inner symbols and meanings is the concretizing of one's own individual symbols by working them out in clay, paints, crayons, collages, pantomime, movement to music, and poetic statement. Artistic criteria should be totally suspended for the time being because most people have been taught too much about what is good and what is bad in art and are thereby handicapped. The ideas of what is beautiful not only are irrelevant here but are actually blocks to a free "letting-happen."

Clay, watercolor paints or finger paints—these are the best media to begin with because they are the most flexible. The medium can be permitted to have its way, for instance, by permitting hands and clay to dialogue with one another, or by "following" a brush (or by getting hands into finger paint) and with color selected at random letting hands, brush, paper, and color carry on a conversation. Each medium has its own unique quality. Clay is the most freeing for many people—especially the untrained—because of its pliability and its willingness to change from shape to shape without resistance. It is also a very satisfying medium to use while listening to music. Finger paints permit great spontaneity, wide movements, and intense colors.

For some, the amount of paint on the hands in itself has a value. Watercolor is less intense but permits of more precision than finger paints. (Other media can be used, but most of them —stone or wood sculpture, oil painting, metalwork, etc.—require more skills initially and do not lend themselves to the faster and freer expressions. Pastels and crayons can be used, however.) For the trained artist, the use of the untrained hand, or dealing with familiar media while the eyes are closed, even blindfolded, has proved very helpful.

What comes from encounters such as these is often surprising, sometimes shocking. Symbolic expressions of unknown parts of a person can emerge spontaneously. He may have to struggle to free himself from lifelong inhibitions and judgments. He must be able to let go of egocentric control as much as possible; he must be able to say, in effect, I don't know what wants to come from inside me and I don't know what it will look like but I am willing to trust that there are things that do want to be expressed. It is as if we had to become like children in order to let out the *rejected inner children* so that they may be brought into the circle of the inner "family."

It is not valuable to try to interpret these symbolic expressions too soon. In fact, there is a danger inherent in trying to do this. It is better to live with what has come out, put it where it can be seen—whether liked or hated—and can be gotten acquainted with as with a strange child who came to visit. For this reason, even when we encourage people to use this free expression method and sometimes in a seminar group the individual expressions are displayed, we ask that people do not interpret one another's work. It must stand as it is until each person begins to know his own "child" better. Only then, shyly, will it reveal its meanings even to its creator.

Another way of using any of the art media for self-exploration is to work with specific images that one has been moved by, or that in some way have taken on significant meanings. Such images may be from a dream, or from a fantasy that has come during a time of meditation. They may be aroused by the hearing of a parable, a poem, music. They may come from myth. We have worked for many years with this method of translating the evoked symbols into personal expression, and have found that no two people express a given image in the same symbolic fashion. This method can be utilized by anyone who is willing to take more or less universal texts (such as a well-known parable, or the myth of the Garden of Eden, or a folktale) and to find some character or scene that is particularly gripping, and then to try to express it *as it feels to him*. What it feels like is what reflects the individual psyche and its projection into the material.

In all work with these symbols as they emerge from the various art media, the results need to be stayed with. It takes inner images a long time to give back all their inherent depth and richness. Their first gift is usually just sheer release, the catharsis of getting out something that has been kept inside. Evil or joyful, it is the same sense of freedom that comes. Slowly, as a person lives with his symbols, he comes to see in them new meanings and he can begin to assimilate those meanings. Only after catharsis and assimilation can he begin to integrate them into growing wholeness and, where it is necessary, transform them. Transformation that comes too soon is forced and is therefore not transformation at all but a flight from truth. These symbolic expressions do many things. They help a person to know that there are unconscious levels of himself. They help him to learn to accept these depths as meaningful and as healing. They lead him to more all-inclusive and accepting attitudes toward himself. In doing all this, they assist him to enter into the "inmost land" where he holds "in balance the globe turning."

20

ONE CONDITION
HAS TO BE MET

*The act of prayer
as continual Yes!*

"Of all the definitions of God," wrote Kazantzakis to his wife, "the one I like best is this one: God is a heart that is upright at the given hour." [96] And the French philosopher Edouard LeRoy wrote:

> Moral and religious reality cannot be perceived without trans-formation of self, without submission of the individual to its exigencies. One condition has to be met; the decision must be taken in advance not only in words but in reality to say "yes" to the light. And this attitude is called prayer. In fact it is prayer even before we realize that we should call it so. [97]

"A heart that is upright. . . ." "In advance . . ." and "in reality to say 'yes' to the light." The upright and affirming heart can face toward the ego (and its concerns of resistances and projections) or toward the various problems arising from deeper unconscious levels. Therefore prayer, "even before we realize that we should call it so," is essential if man is to stay faithfully on this difficult Way. Unless he has some central orientation other than power or gratification or success or comfort, he will forever be pulled on a zigzag course. Resistance to this condition of yes-saying is very great!

There is currently a renaissance of the practice of meditation. We have considered several techniques of meditation. However, unless prayer as defined here precedes or accompanies meditation, there is always the danger of getting lost in the unconscious world of archetypes. What is a minimal definition of prayer? Prayer is the act by which man opens himself to the total values for wholeness that exist in each situational moment of his life. It is an affirmation (reaffirmation) of a fundamental dedication to each moment's emergent highest Value.[98] It assumes the Other, the eternal Thou, as a given. It assumes the presence of a mystery, and of the possibility of grace (the unbidden abundance of God). In the words of the first commandment, prayer is the act of loving God with as much of the all (of heart, soul, strength, mind) as can possibly be brought into consciousness. In contrast to various forms of meditation, prayer is a relationship between the *I*, the situation in which the *I* is functioning, and the Meaning transcending both the *I* and the situation but manifesting itself within both. It is a continual yes-saying to the fact that there is a direction more encompassing than mine, a Purpose larger than mine, for which I can work. It is also a willingness to be open to alternatives, to opposite ways of action or response. When prayer makes this openness possible, it is a marvelous preventer of egocentricity. And this decision to say yes to whatever alternative seems to belong to Purpose must be taken in advance, before any of the specifics of moments are or can be known.

Why is such affirmation necessary? Even the knights of the Grail did not stay on their quest automatically and unerringly. That would not be a realistic picture of the nature of freedom. Freedom requires the possibility of choice which, if it is to be real, means goal-directedness. Goal-directedness means what it says, choosing a goal to move toward. It does not mean a random traveling, now here, now there, on whatever ticket is found in the street to whatever destination may happen.

Prayer is not here defined as "petition"—although we are not ruling out the value of petitionary and intercessory prayer. Our emphasis is on prayer as a ritually repeated statement spoken to the larger Purpose about where we think we are trying to go and why. Such statements can be simple or sophisticated, short or long, ancient or modern, classics spoken by someone else or immediate words coming from one's own heart. Such statements are related to the idea of the holy sentence. For example, from the Atharva-Veda:

> As day and night are not afraid, nor ever suffer
> loss or harm,
> Even so, my spirit, fear not thou.[99]

Or from the Tao-Te King:

> Be bent, and you will remain straight.
> Be vacant, and you will remain full.
> Be worn, and you will remain new.[100]

Then there is this sort of statement, made by Ruth Raymond in her eighty-five-year-old affirmation of the feminine aspect of God:

> I am sure my goddess is being active with and for me, though as
> mysterious as always.
> What is going to become of me is quite mysterious, but I have
> a trustful feeling about it.[101]

Or the words of Mark Pelgrin, facing his death:

> No man can know the ultimate mystery. We never will. But
> a man can invest his life with courage, dignity, sympathy, un-
> derstanding, in such a way as to take the utterly crazy things
> that happen and transform them into a joyful and creative il-

lumination. I am in search of the creativity that is at the center of human-beingness. I cannot know where this lies until I get there, but I have faith it is there where one aspect of God is. All of this implies my dealing with the opposite of what I am used to, a passive and quiet listening to what life (God) says. To learn how to be.[102]

These kinds of prayer are emphases on the conscious act of giving, are efforts of the whole person to deal with partiality and limitation, to give wholly to the process that has been called the "will of God." Sometimes one aspect of the psyche may be dealt with, sometimes another. Sometimes a difficult situation is the focus. Fundamentally, however, in prayer of affirmation one brings into consciousness as much as he knows of himself, of his situation, and he relates it to that teleology overarching his particular point in time and space. It is as if he needed to ask, time after time as life changes its course and as new situations and inner challenges are presented to him, Am I totally *here?* Am I ready for the request? Here I am—where do I go to follow?

Man affirms a goal (nonspecific). He affirms his desire to go there. He brings as much inclusiveness as possible to the going. He confronts purposiveness as it manifests itself in each moment. Within this framework he can deal with specifics. The question now becomes not, *"Am* I willing?" but expands to, *"What must I be willing to do?"*

Earlier we discussed the parable of "importunity," given by Jesus as an answer to a question about prayer. Here we saw that prayer means struggling to understand and to wrest from this Thou its abundance. Now we need to expand this struggle to include what Kierkegaard called the paradox of the "absurd" —the paradox that only through the least-expected, the lowliest, the most offensive parts of oneself does the thrust for wholeness come. Time and again the Other says not only what man does not anticipate but what he does not desire. His "wants" stand over against Its "want." And precisely here, at those times of confusion and conflict as to what is the creative (vs. destructive) action needed, is the place of utmost value for the prayer of affirmation.

In our Western tradition, the prototype of this prayer is that of Jesus when he was struggling to see whether he should or should not enter Jerusalem to face those people who would most probably bring about his death: "Abba, Father, all things are possible to thee; remove this cup from me; yet not what I will, but what thou wilt." (Mark 14:36.) Although it is hard to take this prayer out of the context of the life of Jesus, nonetheless there are certain features of it that can be useful to any person who is struggling for direction.

This is not a prayer of submission. Jesus did not say a resigned, "Your will be done," relinquishing his own desires as if they did not exist. He said that he did have desires and wants— in this case not to drink of the cup of suffering and probable death. He also said that it *could* be that his wants and the wants of God might be the same. But in his final words he affirmed that it was God's Being that must supersede his personal cry. Wholeness lay only in that direction. In so doing he spoke the primary word I-Thou, he set up a dialogue, a "co-creation." Had he denied his own wants, had he ignored the "possible," he would not have been bringing his totality to the situation. Because he had built a new relationship within himself to something that he called "Son of Man," and because he had learned to trust what the Holy Spirit had to say both within him and in outer situations, he could say both "all things are possible," and also "yet not what I will."

Not all prayers of affirmation are dealing with such momentous choices. And yet man can learn from Jesus a significant method for personal use. If periodic reaffirmation of the commitment to God's will as it is revealed in each moment is to have depth of meaning, it needs to include realistically personal needs and the needs of God. In a journal, whenever one is trying to work out what choices to make even in the simple aspects of life, he can write answers to such questions as: What am I trying to decide about? What are my immediate desires? Am I able to let go of these? Am I seeing more than one possibility? Am I open to following whatever seems to be most all-inclusive? Am I being ego-defensive? Ego-repressive? Or can I use my ego strength in the service of the Other, whether within the Self or within the situation? If prayer is worked with in this way, the natural man is not denied, the creative ego not bypassed, nor what comes either from unconscious depths or from consciousness ignored. What one does is to bring all of these together in the inner laboratory as part of the work of wholeness and transformation.

Several things about the ways of working with prayer as a method can enhance its usefulness, things learned from members of experimental seminars over many years. First, we have found that prayer shaped consciously into words seems to be much more valuable for individual growth than if the prayer is left vague. Some people speak the words of their own prayer— or read the words of a written prayer—aloud. Many find that writing down prayers, as well as reading them aloud, makes them more inescapable, and puts the task more urgently.

Paints, crayons, clay can often serve to illuminate the content of prayer. For example, one person often printed his prayer in color, sometimes also drawing around it the things he felt were blocking him. Another modeled in clay what she needed to say yes to.

Music, poetry, or paintings can help to establish the attitude for the yes-saying—especially if distractions tend to interfere with centering down. Most people have some particular musical composition, favorite poem, or painting that brings them quietly into themselves. (Or can discover one.) Such helpers make it easier to begin prayer work.

Regularity (without rigidity) seems to be, for most people, necessary in order to make this affirmative action maximally creative. This means a regular time—with always the openness to change it—and a regular place—even though this may have to be shifted.

Openness. Newness. Freshness. These qualities and attitudes

are essential in all that has been said above. Can each day be approached as a new creation? Can we open ourselves to it, putting into words what may be in the day, of choice, of struggle, of meaning? Can we, each day, again, as if for the first time, move into a center of stillness and say yes? This is prayer—to articulate where we are, to affirm our resolve to respond to God's grace in whatever form It comes, and to see what that requires of us. Then we can move more creatively toward challenges, outer and inner, and can discover also the delight we had not anticipated.

21

A CONDITION
OF COMPLETE SIMPLICITY

*Sacrifice, suffering,
and healing*

At the close of the *Four Quartets,* Eliot says:

> We shall not cease from exploration
> And the end of all our exploring
> Will be to arrive where we started
> And know the place for the first time.
> . . . .
> Quick now, here, now, always—
> A condition of complete simplicity
> (Costing not less than everything)
> And all shall be well and
> All manner of thing shall be well
> When the tongues of flame are in-folded
> Into the crowned knot of fire
> And the fire and the rose are one.[103]

This condition of complete simplicity, this re-turn to the place
of oneself (but with a consciousness about it that one did not

have when he left the garden)—this condition does cost man "not less than everything." Every creative choice he makes involves a letting go of something else. He cannot leave the garden and reenter it simultaneously.

"The distresses of choice are our chance to be blessed," wrote the poet Auden. Every choice involves "distress"—that is, to choose one direction is to have to sacrifice the others; and to sacrifice involves suffering, either neurotic suffering—as when man tries to cling to his cherished defenses at the same time as he is wanting to be loved—or creative suffering, as when he is willing to stand stripped of defenses to face the demands of an unknown Way.

The difference between neurotic suffering and creative suffering is important to know, inasmuch as all too often a person is confused as to which kind he is feeling. Because of this confusion, he can mistake the pangs of his threatened egocentricity for the authenticity of real sacrifice ("Look how I suffer!") and become puffed up. This sends him in the wrong direction, and he tries to avoid the creative pains of seeing how big his defenses are and of consciously letting them be toppled. If we are to mature, the most important sacrifice we must eventually make is the sacrifice of the ego's autonomy. That is to say, the adapted ego, which has ruled for its own sake, has to decide not to rule any longer. It has to choose to serve events and processes larger than itself—those greater-than-ego values in the Self, and in every outer situation. This involves creative suffering and sacrifice. In all the methods described in the preceding sections, clearly this sort of sacrifice is necessary—sacrifice of self-images, of perfection, of being what others desire, of efficiency, of time ordinarily spent on worthwhile outer activity, of being loving. It is perhaps less evident that each of these sacrifices, and any others that must be made for the sake of wholeness, entails suffering of a creative sort, even though the first giving-up often produces neurotic suffering.

For example, if I let go of a self-image that has made me always try to please everyone, I will thereby displease. This causes me neurotic suffering in that I feel I have failed and that I am not loved. However, if I stay with the letting go *in spite* of the neurotic suffering, I will probably come into the creative suffering of knowing that I am like all other people, imperfect, and that therefore, like all others, I will sometimes cause irritation, anger, or inflict pain. This knowledge eventually becomes a healing, or, in the words of the poet, a "chance to be blessed."

What are the kinds of choices that have been set forth in the preceding pages? There is the fundamental and all-inclusive choice of a Way leading to Life. There is a sacrifice of both the support of collective opinion and the comfort of being unconscious. Having chosen to go this Way, man is from thenceforth engaged in a continual process of choosing, sacrificing, suffering, and healing. He becomes aware of more and greater pulls between opposites in the psyche and must learn to discriminate between them, choosing to go sometimes with one, sometimes with another, depending upon *where the Value needs him* (as opposed to where he egocentrically wants to go). Repeatedly he must sacrifice routes that seem direct and "good" for routes that are less direct, more encompassing, and more desirable in the long run.

Once egocentric patterns are seen with any clarity, there is a facing of the ways and means by which to break from these and not stay imprisoned in them. Once the unlived life is glimpsed, man must make choices for those ways in which he can express and integrate this life. These two together—breaking the ego defenses and freeing the unlived life—involve suffering because they usually force one to action against the predetermined and established forms of society in some way or other, as well as against one's own self-images. They also bring great joy of spirit and peace of mind.

A middle-aged man who had worked long and conscientiously at trying to outlast his neurotic suffering and his feelings of martyrdom finally dreamed:

> I am standing in an open place. A great voice coming from everywhere says, "Stop asking who you are and start asking whom you seek."

He had a deep sense of joyful change from this dream, as if, he said in a letter, "I'd been shoved from egocentricity toward who I really could become."

When, in the midst of a period of confessional meditation, a young woman found the words, "You needn't be Hamlet," going around in her mind, she stopped, looked, and laughed at herself suddenly for all her time spent in egocentric distrust and indecision. She saw that she had to give up the protective device of feeling that life was too difficult for her ever to know what to do. She had to stop saying, endlessly, "To be or not to be."

To do seemingly unethical, illegitimate, and unorthodox things is to suffer, as Prometheus suffered for his theft of fire, as Jesus suffered on the cross for his daring to live by the "son of Man" within himself rather than by the Pharisaic law. Renunciation, sacrifice, acceptance of limitation, finitude, and mortality—these lead to a sense of healing, fulfillment, wholeness, and purposiveness. Jung wrote: "The divine process of change manifests itself to our human understanding . . . as punishment, torment, death, and transfiguration." [104] Many are the myths of heroes who sacrifice, suffer, are sacrificed, and bring healing. Many also are the dreams that hold before man's inner eyes the mysteries of sacrifice, pain, and healing. Here are three such dreams. The first, from a man who advanced and retreated too often in his psychological journey, emphasizes the aspect of the sacrifice necessary:

> I stand in front of a large, wooden frame house. I am realizing how beautiful the world would be if in that house lived someone I loved. . . . I seem to converse about this with the voice of the one who orders life, or at least orders my life. Evidently I have asked why I came to this realization only now in my life. "You had to work for it," the voice replied. "If you don't pay fully, you don't know the value of it."

The second dream, from a man who had spent much energy being deeply troubled about the state of the world, and who was beginning to see that he could not save it unless he saved himself, shows how sacrifice (in this case, of a pseudo-scientific pessimism) can point toward healing:

> A man by the side of the road is gathering broad-leafed water plants for healing purposes. I walk through the fields to him to find out how to gather the leaves. It is along a little stream. I look down into a grotto where there is a single large fish in a pool. I think of learning about medicinal herbs to use after the holocaust.

Finally, the dream of a woman in middle life, of European-born parents, illustrates how the abandoned things can yield treasure if we are willing to relinquish our defenses and work with what seems useless:

> I have in my hands a book of the Bible. The cover has been rotted away with age, pages are exposed, and some pages have turned to wood from the long years and weathering from the elements. I wanted to read to some people, but since so much of the book had turned to wood, I pried the pages open. One turned, but it had on it pictures of ancient Egyptian man. Deep in the crevices between two pages, I then found a folded American dollar bill, and when I pulled it out there came a treasure of coins and several pairs of beautiful jeweled earrings.

The historical paradigm of a person who followed this Way to its ultimate end and did not flinch is the life of Jesus, as discussed in this book, and as told in poetry by one of the authors.[105] The sureness with which he moved through his days, encountering enemies, laughing with friends, representing a vital and new kind of being, was a "condition of complete simplicity." It cost him "not less than everything." It marked a new evolutionary mutation of love that only now has a possible chance of altering the direction of Homo sapiens.

It is a real question whether Christianity in its traditional forms can be the expression of this mutation. By projecting onto Jesus most of the mythological qualities of the dying and resurrected gods of the Mediterranean world of his time, Christianity tended to emasculate and rarefy him, diminishing him as a viable paradigm of the evolutionary thrust. Not only has the impact of Jesus been lessened by these projections, but also the rich reservoir of mythic symbols has been covered up insofar as the individual's unconscious depths are concerned. Myths and folktales and dreams, art and imagination have their true reality; Jesus had his of a supranatural magnitude. He was related to his mythic heritage and combined it with his personal evolution, but he should not be identified with it. Perhaps the "new church" as well as the new "non-church" can express the mutation only insofar as they are willing to open themselves both to the unorthodoxy of Jesus and his teachings and also to the illuminating supplementary insights of depth psychology.

One of the central methods, then, if we can call it method, in this long and fruitful journey toward wholeness and the personal incarnation of Meaning is the method of sacrifice, suffering, and healing. This, in Tillich's words [106] involves both an "immediate awareness of something unconditional" and "the courage to take the risk of uncertainty." The awareness of the "unconditional" is an awareness of the fact that there is a "kingdom of God," a "pearl of great price," Life. The courage to "take the risk of uncertainty" is the essence of Freedom and the "free search for ultimate reality."

There are stirring and paradoxical words from one of the ancient Greek mysteries that speak conclusively of the sacrifice-healing relationship and its religious nature:

> The god sent the sickness, was the sickness, was sick, and healed the sickness.[107]

22

THROUGH SOMETHING IN US

Forgiveness as action toward a healing source

In all this long, difficult, exciting journey which man is embarked on, throughout all his efforts—whether in analysis or in the solitude of his own heart—to hear what is calling him and to learn to where it calls him, one need comes again and again. This need is for forgiveness. Man longs to be forgiven. He longs to be able to forgive. Why? Perhaps because forgiveness is, in a very real sense, the process of transformation of his inner and his outer world.

The poet Rilke, in describing the sense of the transitoriness of human life and how man can contain it meaningfully, says:

> These things that live on departure
> understand when you praise them: fleeting, they look for
> rescue through something in us, the most fleeting of all.
> Want us to change them entirely, within our invisible hearts,
> into—oh, endlessly—into ourselves! whosoever we are.[108]

Forgiveness is the rescuing, "through something in us," events and acts from the past that have hurt our neighbor, wounded the Self, and, above all, kept us from hearing God in us. Wounds received and wounds given lead to repressions, deep fears, hostilities, and to a host of lesser demons armed against wholeness. The wounds, given and received, lead also to what in religious language is called "a sense of sin" and in psychological language is called "guilt." We hate ourselves. We hate those who have hurt us so that we hate ourselves. We feel sinful because we hate others. And we feel even more deeply sinful (although for the most part this "sense of sin" is buried) because, through self-hate, we are destroying our most valuable possession, our own selves.

For these reasons, to feel forgiveness may be seen as one of the major goals of working with the techniques we have described. And whether or not a trained healer is involved, forgiveness is both an action of courage and a process of changing inner and outer lives. It is also a matter of remembering, with the psalmist, "If I ascend to heaven, thou art there! If I make my bed in Sheol, thou art there! . . . for darkness is as light with thee." (Ps. 139:8,12.)

The doing of these actions of forgiveness, moreover, requires man to face the fact of sin. To decide to turn in a new direction, and to turn, is in reality to be forgiven.

> When in the middle of sin, in decisionlessness, the will awakes to decision, the integument of ordinary life bursts and the primeval force breaks through and storms upward to heaven.[109]

Another description of this transforming process of forgiveness is at the end of T. S. Eliot's play *Family Reunion:*

> This way the pilgrimage
> Of expiation
> Round and round the circle
> Completing the charm
> So the knot be unknotted
> The cross be uncrossed
> The crooked be made straight. . . .[110]

The psychological problem of forgiveness is seeking for and facing that which must be expiated, that which is knotted and crossed and crooked in both the interior and the exterior life. The religious problem of forgiveness is the bringing of these crooked things into the presence of God, so that they may be accepted, reconciled, and transformed. It is very difficult to take the psychological steps unless the religious factors are also recognized. If man succeeds in opening up the negatives only for the purpose of getting them out, he is in danger either of being possessed by them or of shutting them away again quickly because the pain of them is too great. If he sees them as indications of something new that wants to be born, accepted, and loved, then he can permit them to be, holding them gently despite all their struggling until they can be quieted and changed.

In the synoptic records of the life of Jesus there are several central scenes in which Jesus dealt with the matter of forgiveness. It concerned him. Jesus defined forgiveness as the taking of action in a new direction, i.e., in the words spoken to the paralyzed man (and incidentally to the Pharisees also, who were questioning his dealing with forgiveness):

> For which is easier, to say, "Your sins are forgiven," or to say, "Rise and walk"? (Matt. 9:5.)

In the scene where the prostitute came to him, risking the displeasure of the Pharisee, spending her precious oil and her tears at Jesus' feet, he defined forgiveness as loving action.

> Therefore I tell you, her sins, which are many, are forgiven, for she loved much; but he who is forgiven little, loves little. (Luke 7:47.)

He said another time,

> And forgive us our sins, for we ourselves forgive every one who is indebted to us. (Luke 11:4.)

In this way he linked the action of being forgiven to the action of forgiving. And in the parable that he told when he was being criticized for eating with sinners—the parable of the prodigal son—he defined the forgiveness of the son in the words of the joyous father.

> Bring quickly the best robe, and put it on him; and put a ring on his hand, and shoes on his feet; and bring the fatted calf and kill it, and let us eat and make merry; for this my son was dead, and is alive again; he was lost, and is found. (Luke 15:22–24.)

In all these scenes there is a recognition not only of sin or guilt but also of the presence of something larger than sin or guilt, and an action in a new direction because of this presence.

Where and what is the power that makes for acceptance, turning, forgiveness, healing? It is in what we variously called in this book the Cry, the Meaning, God, existing interiorly (immanently) in the Self, exteriorly (situationally) in man's interrelationships with people and events. It is the teleological thrust toward wholeness and a unitive functioning.

How can one bring oneself into accord with this teleology? In what ways can it be related to? As one of the authors has written:

> I do not think that I forgive. I do not think that we forgive. I think, rather, that the task for me is to bring what I find in myself and in my relationships to that Reality, that eternal Thou, where I can experience forgiving. . . . To say, "I forgive you" has in it always the danger of inflation. I am not the forgiver. I must try to participate in that which is making forgiveness possible. . . . I need to have an "altar," some place where I can feel the Presence, and to that "altar" I can bring whatever I have done to another, or what another has done to me, and there I can feel accepted, forgiven or forgiving, despite what I have done or what has been done to me. . . . What has been done—by me or another—has to be faced, accepted, worked with

lovingly, and thus eventually transformed. And it can be transformed if it is brought to my "altar"—wherever that may be for me.[111]

Most of the ways already described are relevant for work at forgiveness—dialogue, various kinds of meditation, prayer as affirmation, active imagination, art expressions—because each of these ways, plus others, presupposes a conscious and dedicated ego working with Value rather than against it. We would stress three further things relative to forgiveness: the use of symbols that make for reconciliation; the relationship to persons who carry the ability to help man accept himself (including Jesus as a guide toward man's wholeness); the use of the word as it can help man to find the inner authority leading to forgiveness. An example of each of these three things will clarify them.

Wayne G. is possessed by a demon of guilt that renders him helpless whenever he feels he has transgressed the rules of some authority. At such times he hates both himself and the person who is the authority, and then, because of his hate, feels even more guilty. Then he finds a place in the woods near his home where he can go and sit very still and become centered again. Here at his "altar" he learns to bring the sense of guilt and the hate. He learns also how to set them free, without restraint to let them resound through the trees and be "spoken," because they are a part of him and cannot be denied. The words become for him the symbol of the hidden God—and in their protection he can find redemption and reconciliation. (The cross, a great painting, the Yin-Yang circle of the Chinese, and many other symbols can serve in this same way.)

As for relationship to persons, excellent examples of this as a process of forgiveness are found in the life of Jesus and in the way in which, *by a relationship to him,* individuals were helped to rediscover their own identity. Jesus never took upon himself the power of forgiveness. He never said, "I forgive." Always he said, in one way or another, "You are forgiven, because you took that action leading to change." But many times he was the mirror in which persons saw themselves in their creativity and richness. Other religious figures down the ages have also carried some of this quality of being which can help man to accept himself. The analyst represents acceptance. All "significant others" may do the same, to one degree or another. Perhaps in any situation where one has the courage to share with another trusted person one's sense of guilt and need for forgiveness, he may learn to accept the unacceptable.

The use of the word in the process of forgiveness is well exemplified by the following dream of a middle-aged woman who was facing the depth of her own hatreds and hostilities:

> I was in a garden sort of place, big and formal, maybe a palace garden. Coming toward me along a winding walk was a terribly deformed man—crippled, ugly, with an evil face. Before I could get away he grabbed me. He held me in a crushing embrace of his powerful arms, and I knew he was going to kill me. I was paralyzed with fear. Then I began to say the Lord's Prayer. As I said the words, his hold on me grew weaker, and finally his arms fell away. I looked into his face and he was crying like a child.

This woman had brought her hateful and killing side into forgiveness by the use of the word. Following this dream she made this knowledge more conscious, finding that not only such words as those of the prayer but also words from poems, from other writings, even from her own journal, could serve to bring her into the presence of the larger Meaning.

If we have not felt forgiven for our own sins, if we have not accepted the unacceptable in ourselves by acting in a new direction—the direction of inclusiveness of all our parts rather than rejection of them—can we forgive others? Perhaps one of the greatest problems of the good Christian is that he has tried to forgive others without himself feeling forgiven. To see where he has been hurt and then to recognize where, because he has been wounded, he has inflicted pain on others, and finally to see that this endless wheel of being hurt and hurting can be stopped through his willingness to assume responsibility for both sides—this is forgiveness in a man for himself and others.

One further step is necessary. We need to recognize that the Cry must be forgiven for its demanding impatience, as well as that we must be forgiven for not hearing it. There are statements in myth and in religious literature that refer to a "fallibility" in the divine image. For example, in one version of the Navaho Indian creation myth, a central god present from the beginning has the name Wound-in-the-Rainbow, a name which presupposes that the very path of the gods, and the gods themselves, are not perfect, not always all light and flawless. In the magnificent story of Job in the Old Testament, Job says to his wife, after God has permitted Satan to virtually ruin Job's life, "Shall we receive good at the hand of God, and shall we not receive evil?" (Job 2:10.) And later he shouts at God, "Does it seem good to thee to oppress, to despise the work of thy hands and favor the designs of the wicked?" And there are two other statements from Jewish tradition underlining the same theme. In the Midrash, God, speaking of his right and left hands, says, "If I create the world on the basis of mercy alone, its sin will be great; but on the basis of justice alone the world cannot exist." There is also a Jewish legend in which God prays to himself, "May it be My will that My mercy may suppress My anger, and that My compassion may prevail over My other attributes." [112] From the point of view of the divine as well as from the point of view of the human, the movement of forgiveness must be from impatient urgency toward completeness. Rivkah Schärf Kluger [113] speaks of the impossibility of the task to which God set Saul—that of being a prophet and a king (ecstatic/detached and mundane/practical)—another example of why the God-image itself must be forgiven. In the Judeo-Christian tradition, one of the most moving examples of this two-way movement is that of Jesus facing his death on the cross. Before the crucifixion, Jesus brought all his consciousness into his prayer, "All things are possible to thee; remove this cup from me," thus bringing under scrutiny the purposes of God. And his final outcry, "Why hast thou forsaken me?" was a taking onto himself both the dark and light of God. In doing this with courage, and with faithfulness to his own commitment, he brought entirely new dimensions to the meaning of man and to the meaning of Meaning, of God.

Part of the work of forgiveness, in addition to its contribution to the inward transformation process, is what happens in the outer world. As a person struggles with self-acceptance, he inevitably learns to accept others. As he feels forgiveness and love toward his own fallibility, so also can he better love his brother. Reinhold Niebuhr wrote:

> Forgiving love is a possibility only for those who know that they are not good, who feel themselves in need of divine mercy, who live in a dimension deeper and higher than that of moral idealism, feel themselves as well as their fellow men convicted of sin by a holy God and know that the differences between the good man and the bad man are insignificant in his sight. When life is lived in this dimension the chasms which divide men are bridged not directly, not by resolving the conflicts on the historical levels, but by the sense of an ultimate unity in, and common dependence upon, the realm of transcendence. For this reason the religious ideal of forgiveness is more profound and more difficult than the rational virtue of tolerance.[114]

Forgiveness, forgiving, the great to-and-fro movements of Meaning and man between each other—these are the essence of psychic healing. Because man can feel forgiven for the sins that he committed due to his wounds, he can forgive those who wounded him. Also, because he can forgive the wounders (inside him and outside), he can feel forgiven for wounds he has inflicted. Both directions are possible—and healing comes from each—because both are part of the greater Meaning that also wounds and heals.

EPILOGUE

*". . . through the
unknown remembered gate . . ."*

The journey from the Garden of Eden to the Garden of Gethsemane is long and arduous. The journey can be made in the bright twinkling of an eye. It is a journey with markers of "grace." It is a journey of sacrifice and loneliness, bringing man back to an exit that is now a beckoning entrance. It is joy-filled, and shows trees hung with fruits, and deep shade to rest in. The first garden is separated from the second garden by abysses of alienation, of pain, of darkness, and of almost unbearable happiness. A man can turn from the first to the second in a moment of psychological time and pass "through the unknown remembered gate" [115] into a new place of wonder and richness. "But the event that from the side of the world is called turning is called from God's side redemption," wrote Martin Buber.[116]

From what does man turn? To what does he return? When Yahweh dealt with his "disobedient" Adam and Eve, he did not destroy them—which he might have done—nor did he destroy the garden. He left the garden and its trees intact, sent Adam and Eve forth in pain, and set a guard at the open gate back into the garden. Return was therefore assumed to be possible, but those who reentered the garden, past the cherubim with the flaming sword, would have to be different from those who departed in the first place. "Whoever seeks to gain his life will lose it, but whoever loses his life will preserve it." (Luke 17:33.) The first half of this paradox describes man's attempt to cling to the first garden, whereas the second half deals with the turning, the re-turn. Such paradoxes include always the possibility of going around a familiar corner to enter a new place.

C. S. Lewis has described the plight (and opportunity for rebirth) of Adam, thrust from the garden, as the plight (and opportunity for rebirth) of every man who begins to realize his situation and who desires to move into a greater knowing and renewal. The man (Adam) muses on how it must have been, "lying in the sacred turf" as an unconscious "pearl," in a sleepy and motionless universe. Then he says how it is now:

> All this, indeed, I do not remember.
> I remember the remembering, when first waking
> I heard the golden gates behind me
> Fall to, shut fast. On the flinty road,
> Black-frosty, blown on with an eastern wind,
> I found my feet. Forth on a journey,
> Gathering this garment over aching bones,
> I went. I wander still. But the world is round.[117]

On this recognition that the world is round, is always round, is always there for turning, rests man's reborn future. He can, as Adam chose to do, become like one of the gods, knowing both good and evil. He can go forth on a journey. He can, by continuing on this journey, become continually God's imperfect fulfillment. Yahweh's great experiment of entering into time as Freedom can be carried on in no other way than by man's struggles, choices, reversals, and rejoicings. As we said earlier, the happening of consciousness that lies between Eden and

Gethsemane is an enormous happening. And difficult, and unbelievably rewarding because it brings man himself. He can eternally turn again because there is always the larger Purpose to desire him and receive him.

Even in the everyday life of man this turning is redemptive, transformative. He need not wait until the end of his life to recognize this. Time and again he sees, after a period of struggle for consciousness, that he is changed. "I'm not the same person," he says to himself, wonderingly. Or a friend tells him: "You know, you are not like you used to be at all! You've got lots more courage" (or love, or gentleness, or wisdom). After the initial recoil at the thought of how partial he must have been before, he senses that what his friend said is so. Or a dream tells him, as it did to this person:

> I dreamed that I was in my house, but it wasn't my house— I mean, it was changed—and there were new foundations and new walls—it was bigger—and there was a new living room with lots of windows looking out on mountains.

The journeys go on, and each conclusion leads always to another beginning. Not only is this re-turning process intrinsic to an individual's finding of his wholeness, but it is of especial and increasing importance to our Western culture. Eliade points out that in most non-European cultures, historic consciousness hardly exists. But in our Western European (and American) way of life, not only are we aware of history but we are tyrannized and anguished by it because it seems to be headed into a mechanized and meaningless nowhere:

> Judged in the perspective of the primitive religions, the anguish of the modern world is the sign of an imminent death, but of a death that is necessary and redemptive, for it will be followed by a resurrection and the possibility of attaining a new mode of being, that of maturity and responsibility. The end of the world is never absolute; it is always followed by the creation of a new, *regenerated* world.[118]

In the ancient Greek mysteries, there were those who were adopted by the gods. Those were sometimes called *deuteropotmoi* (those to whom a second destiny is given). To be born into "eternal life" is to be reborn, is to have an inner experience of the kind that leads into a different outer existence, one lived on new bases and with expanded reaches. The primitive man's *rite de passage* and the civilized man's *initiation* or *conversion* are in effect the same.

Jesus lived his life in the pattern of the turning and the returning. From the moment that he came to the edge of the Jordan River, heard and responded to John's call to repentance, submitted to baptism, and emerged from this experience with a sense of having been reborn as a beloved son, he walked the path of the turning, of the "reversal." From that point on, through all the wanderings, persecutions, teaching, confrontations with enemies and friends, Jesus chose always to do the act that meant renewal—that meant looking again at the known things and seeing them new. Let us review some of these times of turning in the life of Jesus.

The conclusion of the baptism by John was described as a voice saying, "Thou art my beloved Son; with thee I am well pleased." (Mark 1:11.) Or, "Today I have begotten thee." (Acts 13:33.)

In the wilderness experience,[119] Jesus turned from the current expectations of his people about messianic fulfillment— miraculous acts, or interventions, or assumption of temporal power—and pointed to the realm of God as more all-inclusive than any of these visions of man's realm. This was so great a reversal from tradition that here Jesus began putting his life on the block.

It should be noted in passing that from the time of his baptism experience Jesus manifested the fruits of a turning. He imaginatively re-created an old situation when he equated forgiveness with choosing to move forward. He showed a deepened sense of inner authority when he spoke in the synagogue. There was in him courageous spontaneity, as when he ate with sinners, did not fast when he was filled with joy, picked grain on the

Sabbath because he was hungry. He was able to take the old Jewish laws and reinterpret them, renew them by including the inner processes of wholeness. He stressed over and again that paradox lies at the heart of every choice, that we must let go in order to have, must look into ourselves in order to find what we thought was our brother's problem, must die in order to live.

At the end of his brief life, Jesus returned to Jerusalem to confront the power of those who feared change and were threatened by renewal and rebirth. In the Garden of Gethsemane, Jesus looked at the will of God, held up his own will for consideration, discriminated between the wills, and was able to make the final reversal, the ultimate turning. He prayed

> that, if it were possible, the hour might pass from him. And he said, "Abba, Father, all things are possible to thee; remove this cup from me; yet not what I will, but what thou wilt." (Mark 14:35–36.)

Man's consciousness thus added a vast dimension to the God-man world since the first garden. Eden originally was the garden of quiescent light. Gethsemane was the garden of darkness, choice, and affirmation. The first led to the death of childhood and dependency. The second led to the suffering of the cross, but it also led to a rebirth of love on a scale not possible before. Although Christianity on the whole has failed to deal with the paradoxical reversal religion of Jesus, the life and teachings are there to be examined. Perhaps Jesus, as example of the life of turn and re-turn, can truly come alive only now, in the contemporary world of despair and meaninglessness. Perhaps man's evolution only now is ready to take this next step of "conversion," in which, for each man,

> a second self stands over against the first: a completely new life begins: everything has become different.[120]

Incarnation is an impressive theological word and one that, gripped by contemporary religious fears, people tend to shy away from. Yet is it not really incarnation that is meant by this event called turning? For Meaning to be incarnate is for it to be embodied, to assume a living form or shape, to be manifested in the flesh, to be actualized. For man to turn again, to be reborn, is what the mystics of all times and all faiths have described as man having a sense of the indwelling of God, of man incarnating. The larger Meaning or Purpose can be thus incarnate in each man's psyche. In the words of the poet Rainer Maria Rilke:

> What will you do, God, if Death takes me?
> I am your jug (if someone breaks me?)
> I am your drink (if curdling cakes me?)
> I am your trim, your trade,—it makes me
> think: with me goes your meaning too.[121]

Jung—dealing with the archetypes as patterns of response in the psyche, patterns that manifest themselves in all that man does or does not do, or chooses or does not choose, patterns toward which he must have an attitude of consciousness or they cause him to go against himself—was dealing with "incarnation." If the archetypes are the immanent manifestations of universal Purpose, in this sense they are incarnations, embodiments, indwellings. Through them the Word becomes flesh. And a further step of incarnation must be taken by the individual ego as it chooses how to utilize these archetypal energies. As Jung tells it, by way of paradox:

> Recognition of the archetype . . . forcibly creates the psychological precondition without which redemption would appear meaningless. Redemption does not mean that a burden is taken from one's shoulders which one was never meant to bear. Only the complete person knows how unbearable man is to himself.[122]

It would seem that turning (redemption, rebirth) was seen by Jung as involving incarnation—as almost being synonymous with it—because redemption means carrying the burden of man himself by man himself. The "perfect" (whole) man, he said, must go through the door of the "perfect" man. The Self must be manifested in (embodied in, thus in-carnate in) the very substance of man's life.

One of the reasons Jung was so engrossed in the study of alchemy as having relevance for modern man was because

> in alchemy an attempt was made at a symbolical integration of evil by localizing the divine drama of redemption in man himself.[123]

In the same work he interprets an alchemical treatise as if it were a dream telling the dreamer about the reason for and the nature of the incarnation:

> If you will contemplate your lack of fantasy, of inspiration and inner aliveness, which you feel as sheer stagnation and a barren wilderness, and impregnate it with the interest born of alarm at your inner death, then something can take shape in you, for your inner emptiness conceals just as great a fulness if only you will allow it to penetrate into you. . . . Therefore away with your crude and vulgar desirousness, which childishly and shortsightedly sees only goals within its own narrow horizon. . . . What is behind all this desirousness? A thirsting for the eternal. . . . The more you cling to that which all the world desires, the more you are Everyman, who has not yet discovered himself and stumbles through the world like a blind man leading the blind.[124]

However, man can separate himself from collective opinion and egocentric desire and make a conscious effort to permit the deepest needs of his unconscious psyche to manifest themselves. And this is like discovering and having available a "fountain of renewal."

A sense of Sonship—this has been the mystic's way of trying to say what it feels like when the re-turn has come and the garden has been re-entered through "the unknown remembered gate." In psychological terms it is a sense of Selfhood—of belonging to oneself in the deep belongingness that involves being

under the aegis of a larger-than-self Purpose which is a given.
It is "not what I will, but what thou wilt."

The meaning of Sonship, of Selfhood, can be realized in
many kinds of moments during a life. It can be felt in the simple events of waking, breathing, loving. It can be known ulti-
mately, as when a man is facing death:

> If the coming kingdom is that which made for wholeness in
> me, then God will be pleased in this, his son. I can at this point
> . . . only stumble to find words for this dynamic concept: The
> kingdom within where Self is merged in God is the Kingdom
> where man and God are one . . . the really creative Self is
> always in emergence in all human beings, and death occurs in
> us every day for we must die into the new.[125]

To "die into the new"; to have the Word become flesh and
dwell among us; these movements from a remote there to a
concrete here are also movements that bring into focus the
feminine Godhead, the Mother substance, also there from the
beginning. And so, at the end of each re-turning, the "trinity" of
thrust becomes the "quaternity" of homecoming.

In the first Garden of Eden, the father was there, trying for
manifestation. The son was there also, as soon as the act of
Yahweh brought him (them) into being. And the Holy Spirit
—where was it? Was it embryonically there in the dialogue
between Creator and creatures? Did it reside in part in the subtle
serpent who was the thrust away from paradise? And the fourth
element of the quaternity, the mother, where was she? Perhaps
in the original formlessness. Perhaps also in the longing of the
Lord God for creatures to relate to.

In the life of Jesus this fourfoldness, experienced and understood at the baptism, becomes clearer, and it is easier to see its
operation within man and his psyche. God is the overarching
Meaning to which man commits his total being. Son is what
happens when the commitment is made. Holy Spirit is that
which continually thrusts man forward into wildernesses and
confrontations and all-inclusive existence. Mother is Wisdom,

"justified of all her children," and residing in the frail, loving, suffering, transient flesh. She is the hen who gathers her own brood under her wings.

So we come to the rounding out of this book. Let us once more say, as we did at the beginning, that unless there is choice there is no journey. There is only an exile. The "distresses of choice are our chance to be blessed." Why is this so? And why does man desire this blessing? Why did Jacob risk himself totally in order to receive the blessing? The blessing is, perhaps, this sense of Sonship, of Selfhood, of being related to Meaning, to God, and to the struggles of God. And it is needed today as it always has been—even more than it has been because of the enormity of man's un-blessedness.

REFERENCES and NOTES

1. Paul Tillich, "The Relevance or Irrelevance of Christianity" (Earle Lectures, 1963; on tape at Pacific School of Religion).

2. Pierre Teilhard de Chardin, *The Phenomenon of Man* (Harper & Brothers, 1959); *The Future of Man* (Harper & Row, Publishers, Inc., 1969).

3. "Myth" is used as meaning a symbolic story representing (1) the internal processes of a man's psyche as he struggles for maturity or falls into disintegration; (2) a merging of many such individual processes into an impersonal cultural process, which incorporates the individual's variations into a single body of tradition and ritual. During unstable periods, such as our own, the "myth" is essentially a reflection of individual psychic processes and describes how single persons see their own inner order and meaning. During stable periods of history, the corporate belief, tradition and ritual are parts of a single great myth speaking for all people. Whether the myth is related to one person or to a society, it is made from symbols arising out of the unconscious levels of the psyche. Thus mythology in Joseph Campbell's words is "the revelation to waking consciousness of the powers of its own sustaining source."

4. Rainer Maria Rilke, *Poems from The Book of Hours,* tr. by Babette Deutsch (New Directions, 1941), p. 15.

5. Pierre Teilhard de Chardin, *Building the Earth* (Dimension Books, Inc., 1965).

6. Nikos Kazantzakis, *The Saviors of God* (Simon & Schuster,

Inc., 1960); *Report to Greco* (Simon & Schuster, Inc., 1965).

7. Carl Gustav Jung, *Answer to Job,* in *Psychology and Religion: West and East,* 2d ed., Vol. 11 of *Collected Works* (Princeton University Press, 1969), p. 156.

8. Martin Buber, *I and Thou* (Charles Scribner's Sons, 1967).

9. Jacob Boehme, *Six Theosophic Points* (University of Michigan Press, 1958).

10. Mircea Eliade, *Myths, Dreams, and Mysteries* (Harper & Brothers, 1960), p. 18.

11. Kazantzakis, *The Saviors of God,* p. 91.

12. Carl Gustav Jung, *Mandala Symbolism* (Princeton University Press, 1972).

13. Teilhard de Chardin, *The Phenomenon of Man.*

14. Rhoda Kellogg, *Analyzing Children's Art* (National Press, 1969).

15. W. H. Auden, "New Year Letter (January 1, 1940)," in *Collected Longer Poems* (Random House, Inc., 1941), p. 107.

16. Olaf Stapledon, *Last and First Men* (McGrath Publishing Co., 1930, 1972), p. 326.

17. Ruth Raymond, *We Drew a Circle* (Guild for Psychological Studies, Inc., 2230 Divisadero, San Francisco, Calif. 94115, 1966), p. 106.

18. Mark Pelgrin, . . . *And a Time to Die,* ed. by Sheila Moon and Elizabeth B. Howes (Angel Islands Publications, Inc., 1962), p. 154.

19. Carl Gustav Jung, *Psychology and Alchemy,* 2d ed., Vol. 12 of *Collected Works* (Princeton University Press, 1968), p. 281.

20. Edward Field, "Journey," in *Stand Up, Friend, with Me* (Grove Press, Inc., 1963), p. 45.

21. In subsequent chapters of this book, many of these ideas will be pursued in greater depth. In *The Choice Is Always Ours: An Anthology on the Religious Way,* Revised and Enlarged Edition, edited by Dorothy Berkley Phillips and coedited by Elizabeth Boyden Howes and Lucille M. Nixon (Harper & Brothers, 1960), there are several parts that might be helpful for reference: "Loving God," pp. 88 ff.; "Love," pp. 355 ff.; "Some Modern Ideas of God," pp. 395 ff.

22. Joshua Loth Liebman, *Peace of Mind* (Simon & Schuster, Inc., 1949).

23. Martin Buber, *I and Thou,* p. 46.

24. Teilhard de Chardin, *The Phenomenon of Man,* p. 259.

25. Fritz Kunkel, *In Search of Maturity* (Charles Scribner's Sons, 1943).

26. Frances Wickes, *The Inner World of Choice* (Harper & Row, Publishers, Inc., 1963), pp. 20–21.

27. Mircea Eliade, *Myth of the Eternal Return* (Princeton University Press, 1954).

28. It should be kept in mind that the words "symbol," "myth," "archetype," are used to refer to ways in which events in the *inner* world of a person are manifested to his *outer* world. To oversimplify, a *symbol* is a literal reference which carries a much fuller range of meanings and emotions than that to which it refers. A *myth* is a story telling of the operations and interrelationships of those archetypes involved in man's behavior and beliefs. *Archetypes* are primary patterns of human behavior which have more or less universal and instinctual manifestations and are often seen through their symbolic and/or mythic content.

29. Carl Gustav Jung, *Integration of Personality* (Farrar & Rinehart, Inc., 1939), pp. 288–289, 302.

30. Martin Buber, *Between Man and Man* (Beacon Press, Inc., 1953), p. 25.

31. Emily Dickinson, "The Heart is the Capital of the Mind," in *The Complete Poems of Emily Dickinson,* ed. by Thomas H. Johnson (Little, Brown & Company, 1945), p. 346.

32. Erich Neumann, *Origins and History of Consciousness* (Princeton University Press, 1970).

33. Elizabeth Boyden Howes, *Intersection and Beyond* (Guild for Psychological Studies, Inc., 2230 Divisadero, San Francisco, Calif. 94115, 1971), pp. 3 ff.

34. Maria Leach, *The Beginning: Creation Myths Around the World* (Funk & Wagnalls Company, 1956), p. 58.

35. *Ibid.,* p. 61.

36. Aniela Jaffé, *The Myth of Meaning* (G. P. Putnam's Sons, 1971).

37. Fritz Kunkel, *How Character Develops* (Charles Scribner's Sons, 1940); *In Search of Maturity.*

38. Charles Williams, *House by the Stable,* in *Collected Plays* (London: Oxford University Press, 1963), pp. 201, 202.

39. Sheila Moon, *A Magic Dwells: A Poetic and Psychological Study of the Navaho Emergence Myth* (Wesleyan University Press, 1970).

40. Carl Gustav Jung, *Mysterium Coniunctionis*, 2d ed., Vol. 14 of *Collected Works* (Princeton University Press, 1970), p. 272.

41. Helmuth Jacobsohn *et al.*, *Timeless Documents of the Soul* (Northwestern University Press, 1968), p. 44.

42. For some of the best discussions of archetypes, see: Jolande Jacobi, *Complex, Archetype, Symbol in the Psychology of C. G. Jung* (Pantheon Books, 1959); Carl Gustav Jung, *Archetypes and the Collective Unconscious,* 2d ed., Vol. 9, Part I, of *Collected Works* (Princeton University Press, 1968); Joseph Campbell, *Hero with a Thousand Faces,* rev. ed. (Princeton University Press, 1968), 4 vols. on mythology; Carl Gustav Jung (ed.), *Man and His Symbols* (Doubleday & Co., Inc., 1964); *The Archetype* (Proceedings of 2d International Congress of Analytical Psychology, Zurich, 1962).

43. Dante, *The Divine Comedy,* Inferno, V, 48–51.

44. Leland C. Wyman (ed.), *Beautyway: A Navaho Ceremonial,* tr. by Fr. Berard Haile (Pantheon Books, 1957). See statement concerning his original text in Moon, *A Magic Dwells,* p. 82.

45. Max Dimont, *Jews, God and History* (Simon & Schuster, Inc., 1962).

46. Carl G. Jung, *The Undiscovered Self* (Little, Brown & Company, 1958); *Answer to Job; Essays on Contemporary Events* (Routledge & Kegan Paul, Ltd., 1947).

47. Victor White, *God and the Unconscious* (Henry Regnery Company, 1953).

48. Liliane Frey-Rohn, "Evil from the Psychological Point of View," in *Evil: Studies in Jungian Thought* (Northwestern University Press, 1967), p. 186.

49. Gerardus van der Leeuw, *Religion in Essence and Manifestation* (Peter Smith Publisher, Inc., n.d.), p. 359.

50. Howes, *op. cit.,* p. 47.

51. Jung, *Psychology and Religion,* p. 262.

52. Sir Gawain, in *King Arthur and His Knights of the Round Table* (Penguin Books, Inc., 1953).

53. Portion of Jeremiah, ch. 15, quoted also in "The Inward Renewal" section of Phillips (ed.), *op. cit.,* p. 335.

54. William Soutar, "From the Wilderness," in *Collected Poems,*
ed. by Hugh Macdiarmid (London: Andrew Dakers, Ltd., 1948).

55. Erich Neumann, "Art and Time," in *Papers from the Eranos
Yearbooks* (Princeton University Press, 1970), p. 43.

56. T. S. Eliot, *Four Quartets* (Harcourt, Brace and Company,
Inc., 1952), pp. 11, 17.

57. Mary Caroline Richards, *Centering in Pottery, Poetry and
the Person* (Wesleyan University Press, 1964), p. 36.

58. Theodosius Dobzhansky, *Biology of Ultimate Concern* (The
New American Library of World Literature, Inc., 1967), p. 130.

59. Paul Reps (comp.), *Zen Flesh, Zen Bones* (Charles E. Tut-
tle Co., Inc., 1957), pp. 111, 123.

60. Denise Levertov, "Joy," in *The Sorrow Dance* (New Directions Publishing Corp., 1967), p. 33.

61. Kazantzakis, *The Saviors of God,* pp. 63–64, 78–79.

62. Rollo May, in *San Francisco Chronicle,* Nov. 29, 1968.

63. Raymond, *op. cit.,* p. 35.

64. T. S. Eliot, *Family Reunion* (Harcourt, Brace and Company,
Inc., 1939), pp. 275, 281.

65. Juliana of Norwich, *Revelations of Divine Love* (The New-
man Press, 1952).

66. Nikos Kazantzakis, *Zorba the Greek* (Simon & Schuster,
Inc., 1961), p. 300.

67. Margaret Schevill Link, *The Pollen Path* (Stanford University Press, 1956), p. 72.

68. William Law, *A Serious Call to a Devout and Holy Life*
(Wm. E. Eerdmans Publishing Co., n.d.).

69. Kunkel, *How Character Develops.*

70. C. F. Lummis, *Pueblo Indian Folk Stories* (Century Company, 1910).

71. Lewis Spence, *Myths and Legends: The North American Indians* (Nickerson, n.d.).

72. Josephine W. Johnson, "Let Go. Return," in *Year's End*
(Simon & Schuster, Inc., 1937), p. 6.

73. Phillips (ed.), *op. cit.,* pp. 42–63.

74. Brother Antoninus, "A Frost Lay White on California," in
The Hazards of Holiness: Poems, 1957–1960 (Doubleday & Company, Inc., 1962), p. 38.

75. Link, *op. cit.,* p. 76.

76. Linda Fierz-David, Unpublished notes.

77. Some of these teachers with whom the authors have had a working experience are Hildegard Elsberg and Magdalene Proskauer, both of San Francisco, and Charlotte Selver-Brooks, of New York City. All of them have had their training under the master teachers in Europe and are sound in their knowledge.

78. Jaffé, *op. cit.;* Carl Gustav Jung, *Structure and Dynamics of the Psyche,* 2d ed., *Collected Works,* Vol. 8 (Princeton University Press, 1969).

79. William Carlos Williams, "Danse Russe," in *Collected Earlier Poems* (New Directions Publishing Corp., 1938), p. 148.

80. Gerald Heard, *These Hurrying Years* (Oxford University Press, 1931).

81. William Shakespeare, *Othello,* Act I, Scene III; Act IV, Scene II.

82. Culver Barker, Unpublished lecture.

83. Kunkel, *How Character Develops,* p. 28.

84. Gerhard Adler, "Methods of Treatment in Analytical Psychology," in Benjamin B. Wolman, *Psychoanalytic Techniques* (Basic Books, Inc., 1967), p. 345.

85. May Sarton, "On Being Given Time," in *Cloud, Stone, Sun, Vine* (W. W. Norton & Company, Inc., 1961), p. 59.

86. C. A. Meier, *Ancient Incubation and Modern Psychotherapy* (Northwestern University Press, 1967).

87. Evelyn Underhill, *Mysticism* (E. P. Dutton & Co., Inc., 1955).

88. William Johnston, *The Still Point* (Harper & Row, Publishers, Inc., 1970).

89. Phillips (ed.), *op. cit.*

90. Brother Lawrence, *The Practice of the Presence of God.* In many editions.

91. Kunkel, *In Search of Maturity,* p. 79.

92. Hans Schaer, *Religion and the Cure of Souls in Jung's Psychology* (Pantheon Books, 1950).

93. Barbara Hannah, "On Active Imagination," in *Spring Magazine,* 1953, and in many unpublished lectures.

94. Gerhard Adler, *The Living Symbol* (Princeton University Press, 1961).

95. Carl Gustav Jung, *The Secret of the Golden Flower,* in

Alchemical Studies, Collected Works, Vol. 13 (Princeton University Press, 1967).

96. Helen N. Kazantzakis, *Nikos Kazantzakis: A Biography Based on His Letters* (Simon & Schuster, Inc., 1968), p. 141.

97. Edouard LeRoy, *Le Problème de Dieu,* tr. by Dora Wilson, as quoted in Phillips (ed.), *op. cit.,* p. 159.

98. For a full presentation of "The Object of Devotion," see the appendix bearing this title in Phillips (ed.), *The Choice Is Always Ours,* pp. 393 ff.

99. Atharva-Veda, *The Bible of the World,* ed. by Robert O. Ballou (The Viking Press, Inc., 1939), p. 23.

100. Tao-Te King, *ibid.,* p. 326.

101. Raymond, *op. cit.,* p. 78.

102. Pelgrin, *op. cit.,* p. 128.

103. Eliot, *Four Quartets,* p. 39.

104. Jung, *Alchemical Studies.*

105. Sheila Moon, *Joseph's Son* (Golden Quill Press, 1972).

106. Paul Tillich, *Biblical Religion and the Search for Ultimate Reality* (The University of Chicago Press, 1955), p. 153.

107. C. A. Meier, "Ancient Incubation and Modern Psychotherapy," in *Spring Magazine,* 1953, p. 60. See also "He was the sickness and the remedy . . ." in Dr. Meier's *Ancient Incubation and Modern Psychotherapy.*

108. Rainer Maria Rilke, *Duino Elegies,* tr. from the German by J. B. Leishman and Stephen Spender (W. W. Norton & Company, Inc., 1939), p. 77.

109. Martin Buber, quoted in Maurice Stanley Friedman, *Martin Buber: The Life of Dialogue* (Harper & Brothers, 1960), p. 33.

110. Eliot, *Family Reunion,* p. 131.

111. Howes, *op. cit.,* p. 58.

112. Midrash and Jewish legend, quoted in Carl Gustav Jung, *Aion: Researches Into the Phenomenology of the Self,* 2d ed., Vol. 9, Part II, of *Collected Works* (Princeton University Press, 1968), pp. 59–60.

113. Rivkah Schärf Kluger, "King Saul and the Spirit of God," in *Spring Magazine,* 1948.

114. Reinhold Niebuhr, *An Interpretation of Christian Ethics* (Harper & Brothers, 1935), p. 226.

115. Eliot, *Four Quartets,* p. 239.

116. Buber, *I and Thou*, p. 120.

117. C. S. Lewis, "Poem for Psychoanalysts and/or Theologians," in *Poems*, ed. by Walter Hooper (Harcourt Brace Jovanovich, Inc., 1964), p. 192.

118. Van der Leeuw, *op. cit.*, p. 159.

119. See Matt. 4:1–11; Mark 1:12–13; Luke 4:1–13.

120. Van der Leeuw, *op. cit.*, p. 533.

121. Rainer Maria Rilke, "What will you do, God, if Death takes me?" in *Selected Works*, Vol. II, tr. by J. B. Leishman (New Directions Publishing Corp., 1960), p. 43.

122. Jung, *Aion*, p. 70.

123. Jung, *Mysterium Coniunctionis*, p. 451.

124. *Ibid.*, pp. 160–162.

125. Pelgrin, *op. cit.*, p. 141.

INDEX